101 SCIENCE TRICKS

FUN EXPERIMENTS WITH EVERYDAY MATERIALS

ROY RICHARDS

Illustrated by Alex Pang

SIMON & SCHUSTER

LONDON • SYDNEY • NEW YORK • TOKYO • SINGAPORE • TORONTO

CONTENTS

3 **On Paper**

For Phoebe Jane

First published in 1990
by Simon & Schuster Young Books

Reprinted 1992

Simon & Schuster Young Books
Campus 400
Maylands Avenue
Hemel Hempstead, Herts HP2 7EZ

Text © 1990 Roy Richards
Illustrations © 1990 Simon & Schuster

Printed and bound in Hong Kong by Wing King Tong Co. Ltd.

British Library Cataloguing in Publication Data
Richards, Roy
    101 science tricks.
    1. Science, Experiments
    I. Title
    507.24

    ISBN 0-7500-0281-6
    ISBN 0-7500-0556-4 Pbk.

1
on Looking

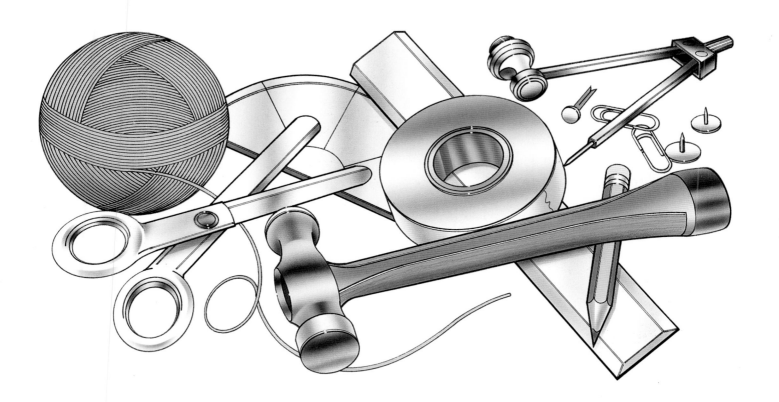

INTRODUCTION

People say that seeing is believing, but have you ever really thought about the way you see things? Sometimes things aren't what they seem! In **On Looking** you'll find lots of fun experiments to do with mirrors and with the way you see things. Did you know that you can use mirrors to make a periscope to peep over the garden wall and around corners to find out what is happening? That's just what a submarine does. It raises a special tube called a periscope up out of the water to find out what is happening without being seen. How about surprising your friends with some optical illusions and designs. There are lots of things that you can do to make pictures move. The Victorians used to enjoy moving picture toys and you too can make some of these. You can get a dancer waltzing, a frog leaping or a dolphin jumping. Did you know that these moving pictures were the beginning of cinema? The Victorians would sit in their parlours on a Sunday and watch them! These things to do are all about creating illusions but there are lots of other ways of creating illusions to surprise your friends.

You will find that it is easy to see from the illustrations and the instructions what you need to make the things, but to help you a comprehensive list of all the materials needed is given on page 101.

MIRROR PLAY

Use a mirror.

1 Look at the sky. Be careful. Do not look at the sun.

2 Look around corners with your mirror.

3 Look behind you. What can you see.

4 Use your mirror to look over walls.

5 Write your name on a large piece of paper. Look at it in a mirror.

JUST ONE MIRROR

Take a handbag mirror.

Put it along each dotted line in turn, shiny side facing each picture, as shown in the picture on the left. What happens?

Make some designs of your own.

Put your mirror here.

DICK
MARY

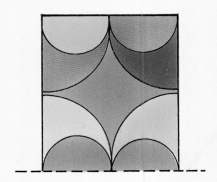

1 Try your mirror on letters.

2 Examine the letters of the alphabet below. Which have vertical symmetry? Which have horizontal symmetry? Which have both? Which have none? Use the letters that show symmetry to make symmetrical words as shown below at the bottom of the page.

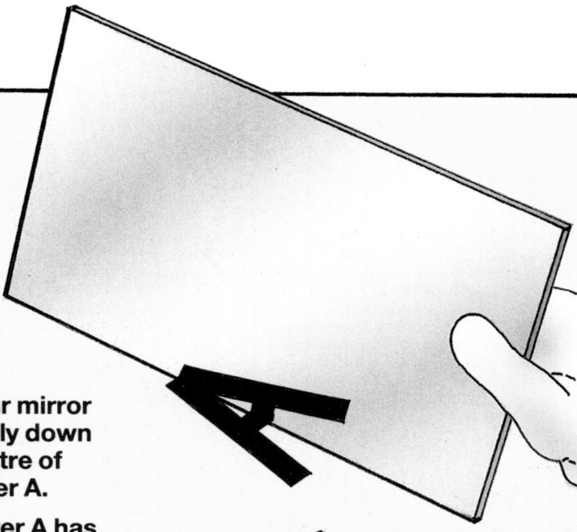

Put your mirror vertically down the centre of the letter A.

The letter A has vertical symmetry.

Try it on the letter B.

It does not work for the letter B.

ABCDE
FGHIJK
LMNOP
QRSTU
VWXYZ

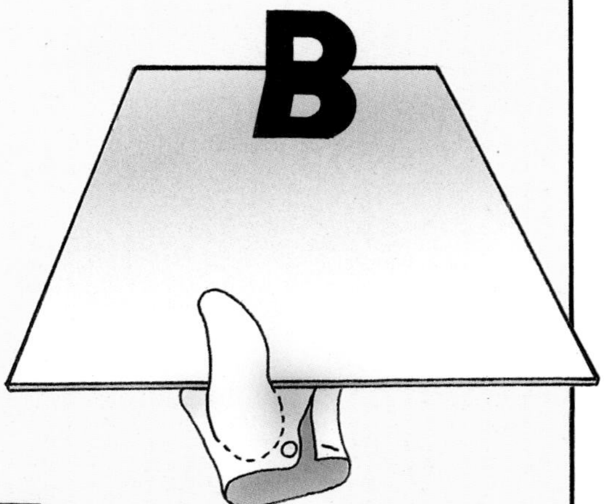

HAT

MUM

symmetrical words

Try the mirror horizontally across the letter B.

Now it works! The letter B has horizontal symmetry.

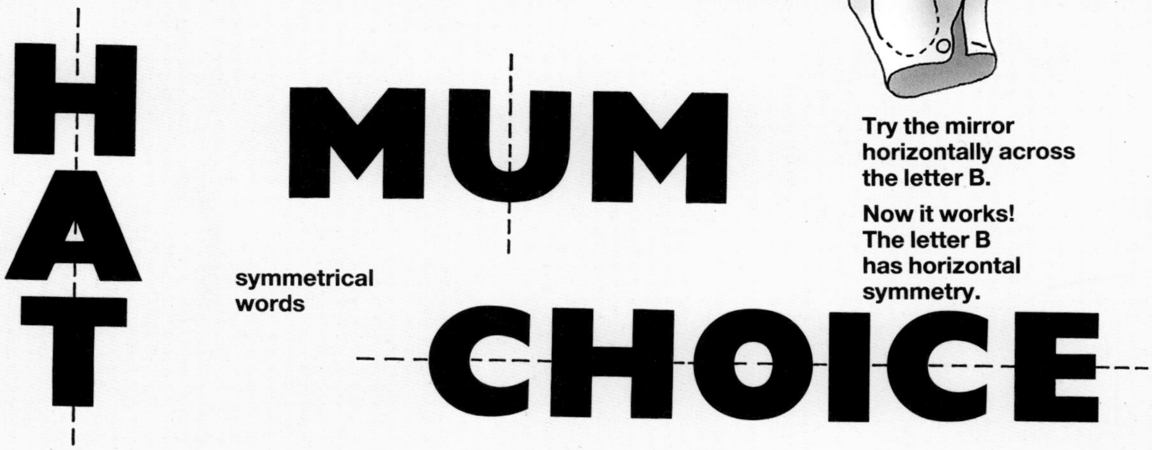

CHOICE

TRY TWO MIRRORS

1 Join two mirrors with sticky tape as below.

2 Stand them up with the mirror fronts facing you.

3 Try your mirrors on each tortoise in turn. Place the mirrors on the dotted lines as shown, shiny sides facing on the tortoise. What happens? Now try these patterns.

place your mirrors here, shiny sides facing tortoise

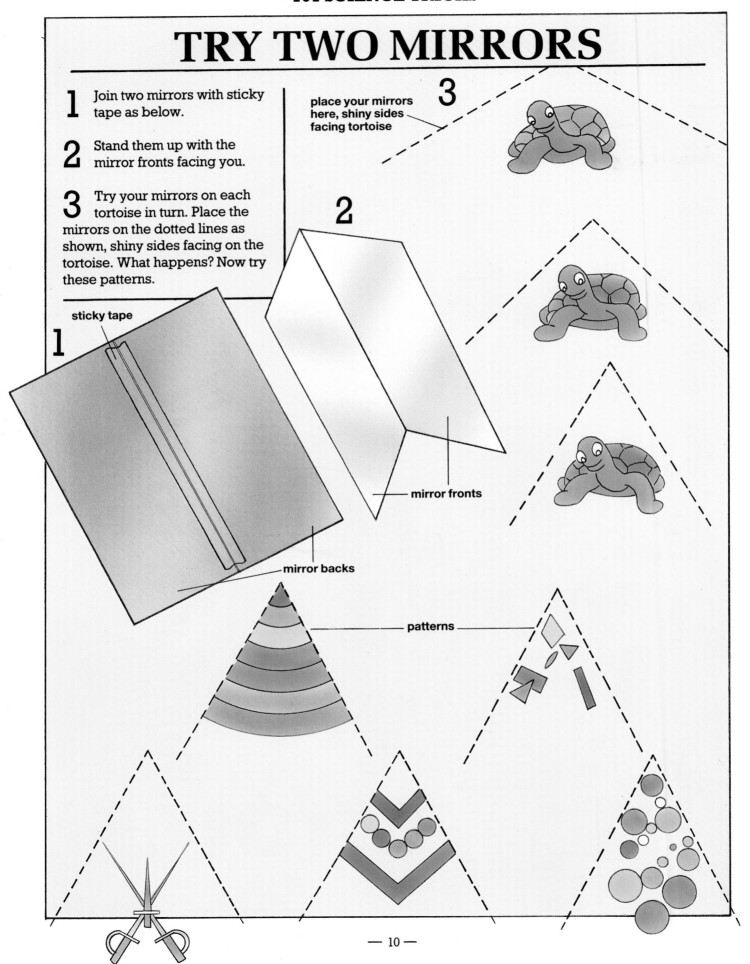

sticky tape

mirror fronts

mirror backs

patterns

KALEIDOSCOPE

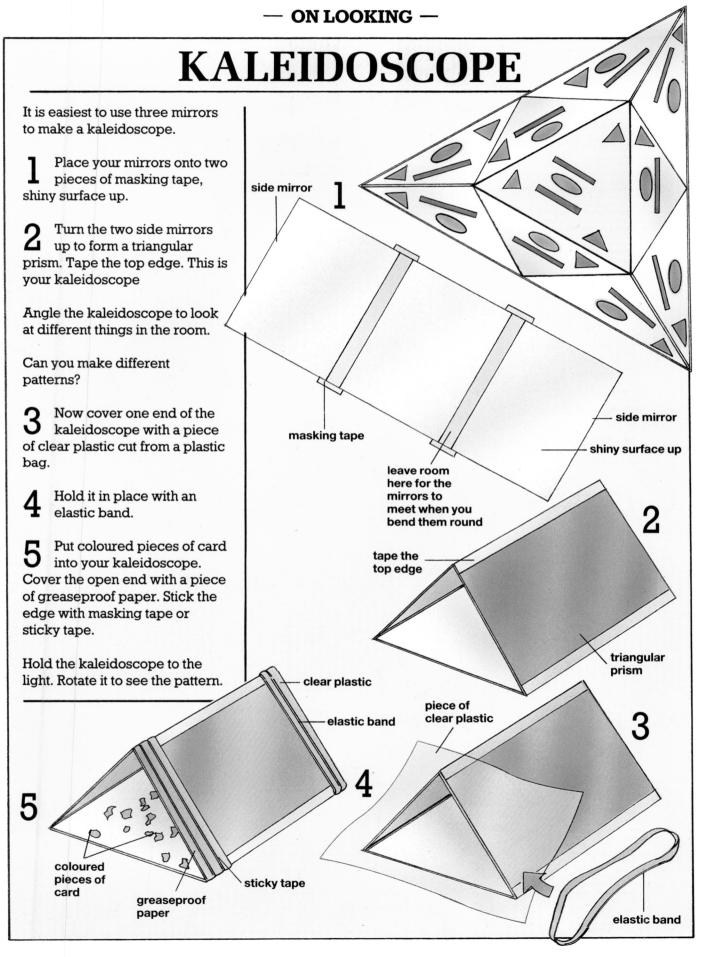

It is easiest to use three mirrors to make a kaleidoscope.

1 Place your mirrors onto two pieces of masking tape, shiny surface up.

2 Turn the two side mirrors up to form a triangular prism. Tape the top edge. This is your kaleidoscope

Angle the kaleidoscope to look at different things in the room.

Can you make different patterns?

3 Now cover one end of the kaleidoscope with a piece of clear plastic cut from a plastic bag.

4 Hold it in place with an elastic band.

5 Put coloured pieces of card into your kaleidoscope. Cover the open end with a piece of greaseproof paper. Stick the edge with masking tape or sticky tape.

Hold the kaleidoscope to the light. Rotate it to see the pattern.

side mirror

masking tape

leave room here for the mirrors to meet when you bend them round

side mirror

shiny surface up

tape the top edge

triangular prism

clear plastic

elastic band

piece of clear plastic

coloured pieces of card

greaseproof paper

sticky tape

elastic band

PERISCOPES

Periscopes can be used to peep over walls or around corners. They can also be used to watch processions.

You will need two handbag mirrors to make a periscope and some long pieces of card.

1 Cut a long piece of card about 2½ times as long as the mirror but just as wide. Tape one of your mirrors to the middle of the piece of card, with the shiny surface facing up.

2 Fold the card into a triangular prism. Make sure you have a 90 degree angle at one corner. You may have a slight overlap in the card. Tape this overlap.

3 Do the same thing with your other mirror.

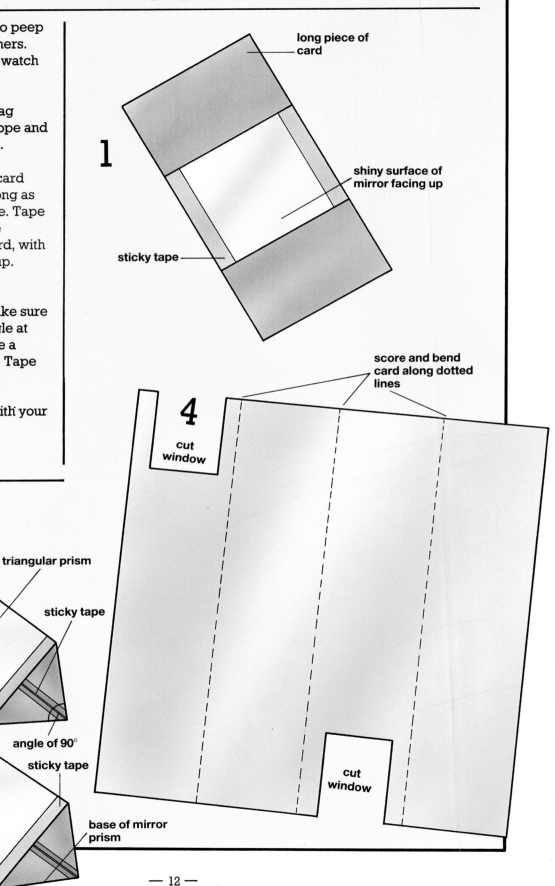

1

long piece of card

shiny surface of mirror facing up

sticky tape

4

score and bend card along dotted lines

cut window

cut window

2

triangular prism

sticky tape

shiny surfaces of mirrors

angle of 90°

3

sticky tape

base of mirror prism

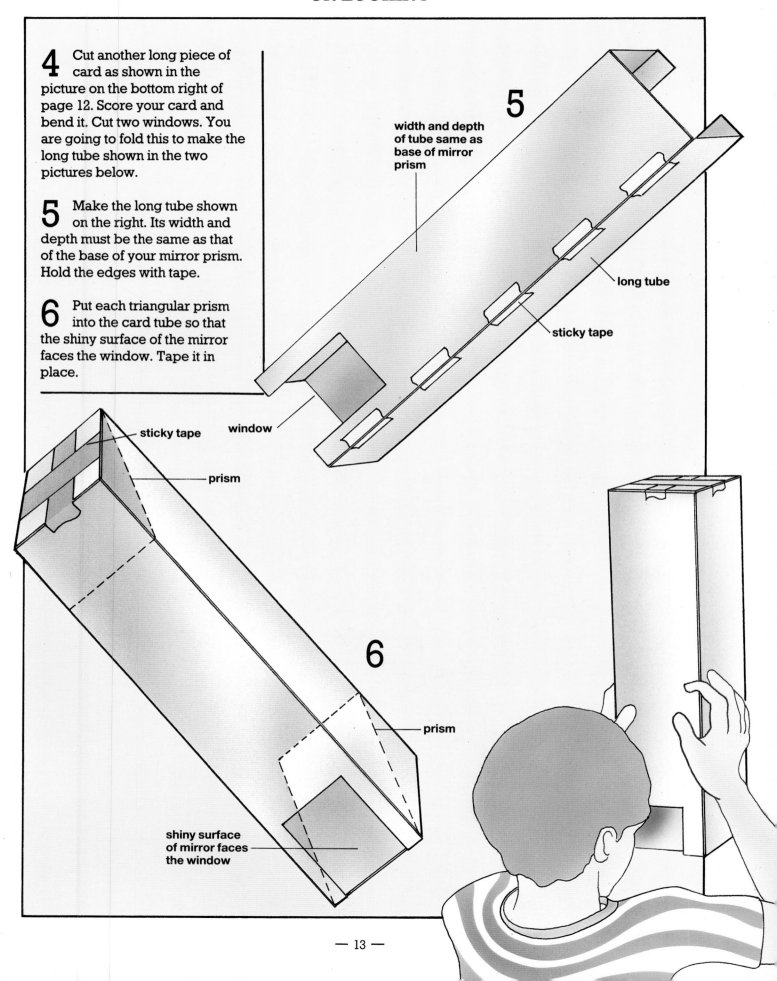

4 Cut another long piece of card as shown in the picture on the bottom right of page 12. Score your card and bend it. Cut two windows. You are going to fold this to make the long tube shown in the two pictures below.

5 Make the long tube shown on the right. Its width and depth must be the same as that of the base of your mirror prism. Hold the edges with tape.

6 Put each triangular prism into the card tube so that the shiny surface of the mirror faces the window. Tape it in place.

5

width and depth of tube same as base of mirror prism

long tube

sticky tape

window

sticky tape

prism

6

prism

shiny surface of mirror faces the window

SEEING IS BELIEVING

1 Cut out a piece of card the same size as the one immediately below.

2 Place your card vertically along the dotted line between each of the pictures below. Put your nose on the top edge of the card as shown in the picture on the right. What happens?

Each eye receives a separate image. The brain merges these two images to make one picture. So the rabbit pops into its hutch or the spider into its web.

card

70mm

45mm

place your card vertically along the dotted line

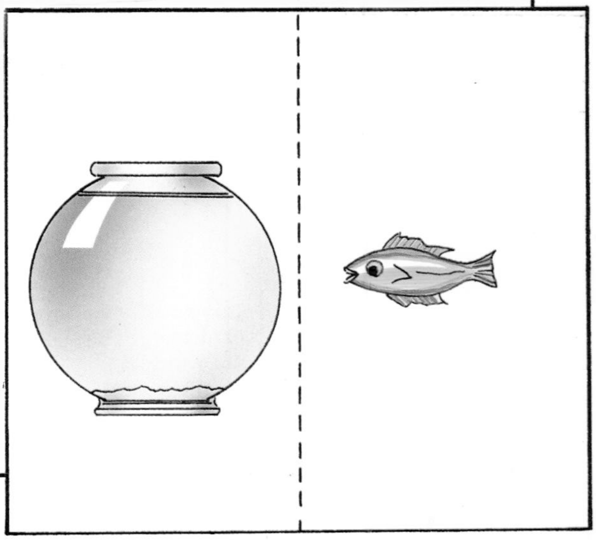

Make up some illusion cards.

Try them on your friends.

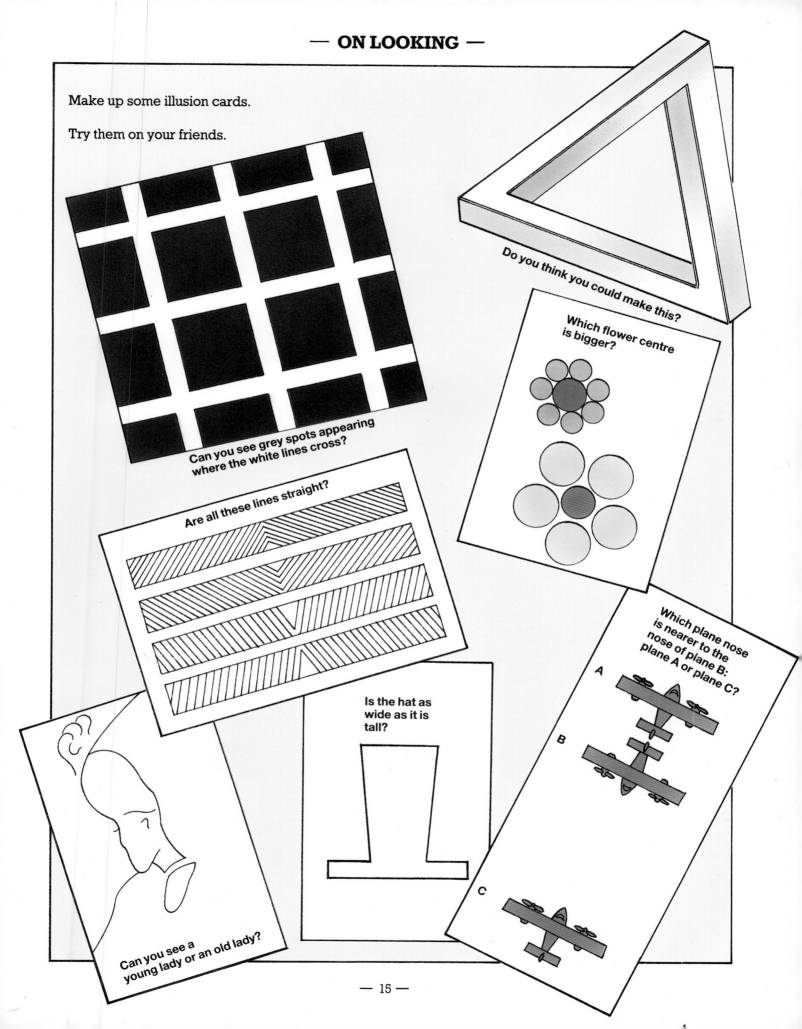

Can you see grey spots appearing where the white lines cross?

Do you think you could make this?

Which flower centre is bigger?

Are all these lines straight?

Which plane nose is nearer to the nose of plane B: plane A or plane C?

A

B

C

Is the hat as wide as it is tall?

Can you see a young lady or an old lady?

THAUMATROPES

The thaumatrope was invented in 1826 and is one of the earliest optical toys. It is a spinning disc with a picture either side.

1 Cut a disc sixty millimetres in diameter from card.

2 Punch holes near the edge of the card.

3 Thread string through the holes of the card.

4 Draw pictures on each side of the card circle. Remember to have the back picture upside down as shown.

5 Turn the strings. The two pictures will merge as you spin the disc.

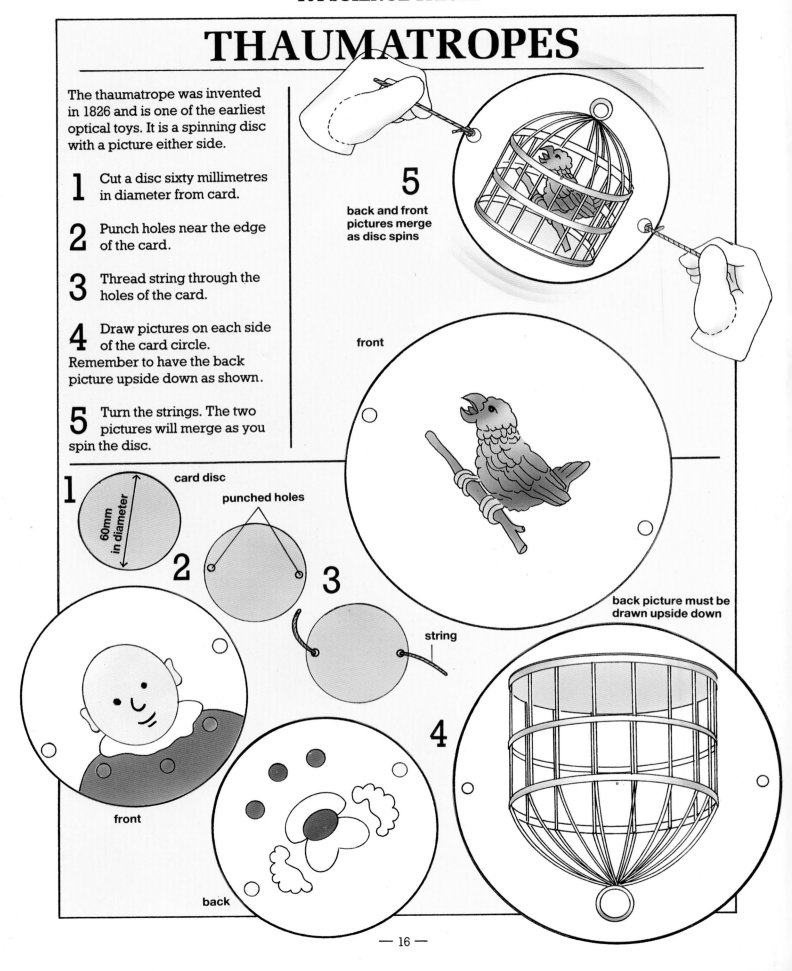

5 back and front pictures merge as disc spins

front

1 card disc
60mm in diameter

2 punched holes

3 string

4 back picture must be drawn upside down

front

back

punch holes for string

You can also use card oblongs. Here are more suggestions for designs for you to copy or trace.

card oblong

and rider

horse

and tiger

stripes

and sunglasses

eyes

PHENAKISTOSCOPES

Joseph Antoine Plateau, a Belgian discovered an intriguing effect produced by viewing moving pictures through slits.

The device he invented was called a phenakistoscope or stroboscope. The way this works is because the brain has the

ability to retain pictures for a short while. Each successive picture of the frog stays in your mind.

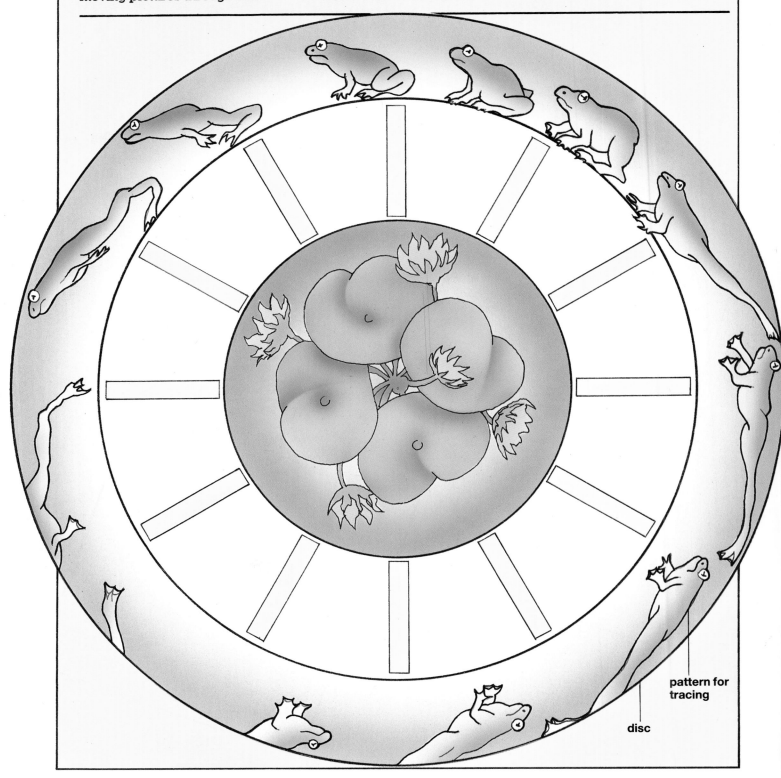

pattern for tracing

disc

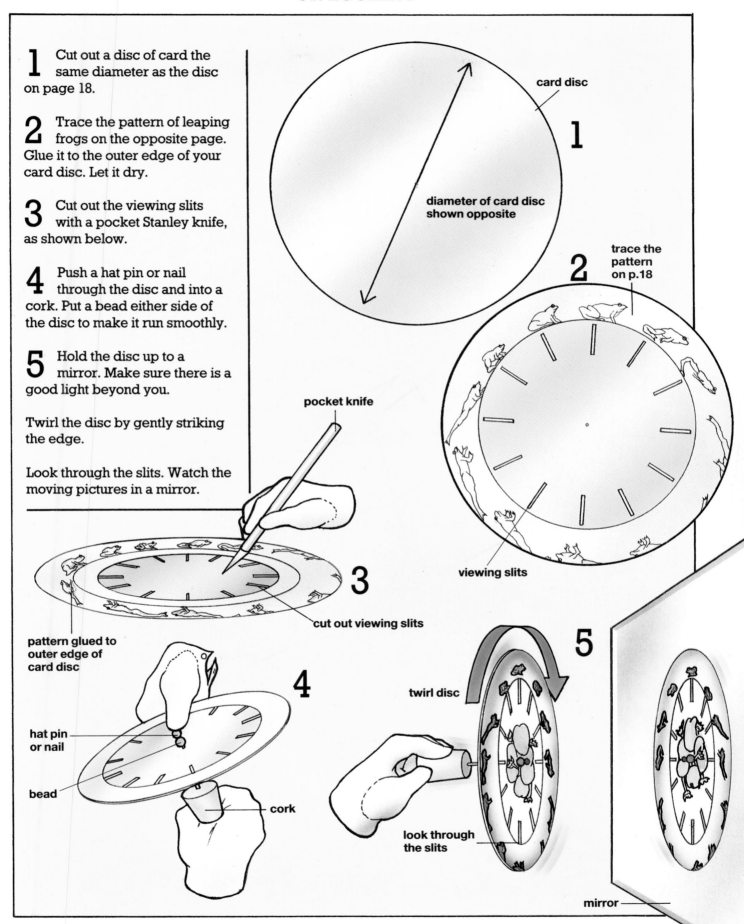

1 Cut out a disc of card the same diameter as the disc on page 18.

2 Trace the pattern of leaping frogs on the opposite page. Glue it to the outer edge of your card disc. Let it dry.

3 Cut out the viewing slits with a pocket Stanley knife, as shown below.

4 Push a hat pin or nail through the disc and into a cork. Put a bead either side of the disc to make it run smoothly.

5 Hold the disc up to a mirror. Make sure there is a good light beyond you.

Twirl the disc by gently striking the edge.

Look through the slits. Watch the moving pictures in a mirror.

card disc

diameter of card disc shown opposite

1

trace the pattern on p.18

2

viewing slits

pocket knife

pattern glued to outer edge of card disc

cut out viewing slits

3

hat pin or nail

bead

cork

4

twirl disc

look through the slits

5

mirror

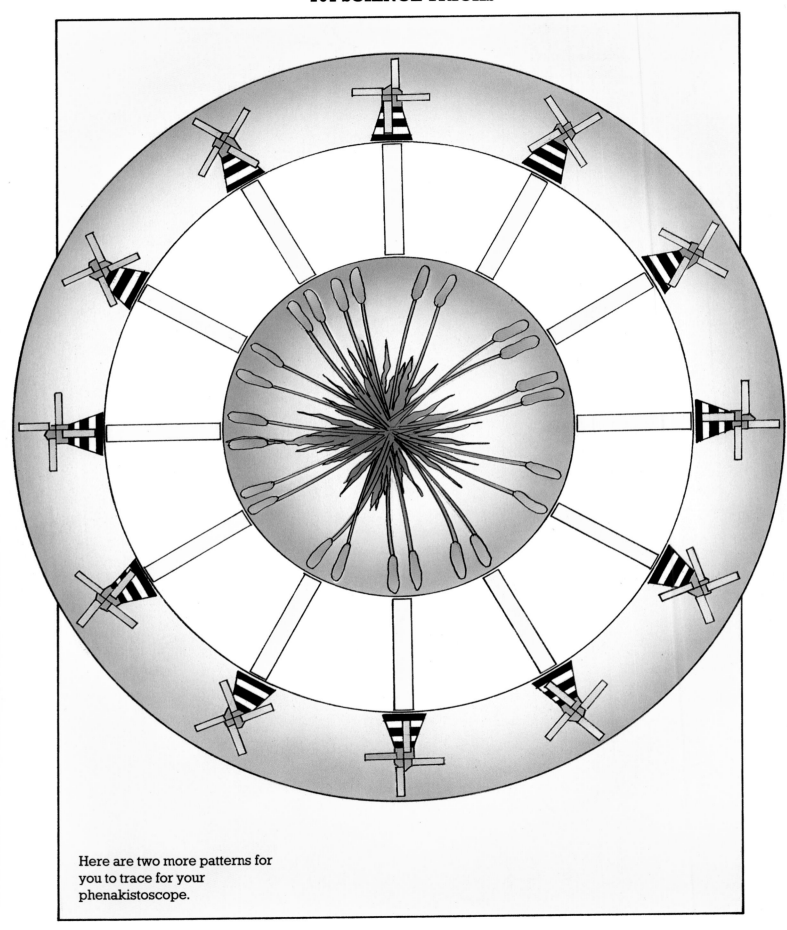

Here are two more patterns for you to trace for your phenakistoscope.

Try viewing through the slits whilst spinning the disc slowly.

Now try viewing but spin the disc quickly.

What happens?

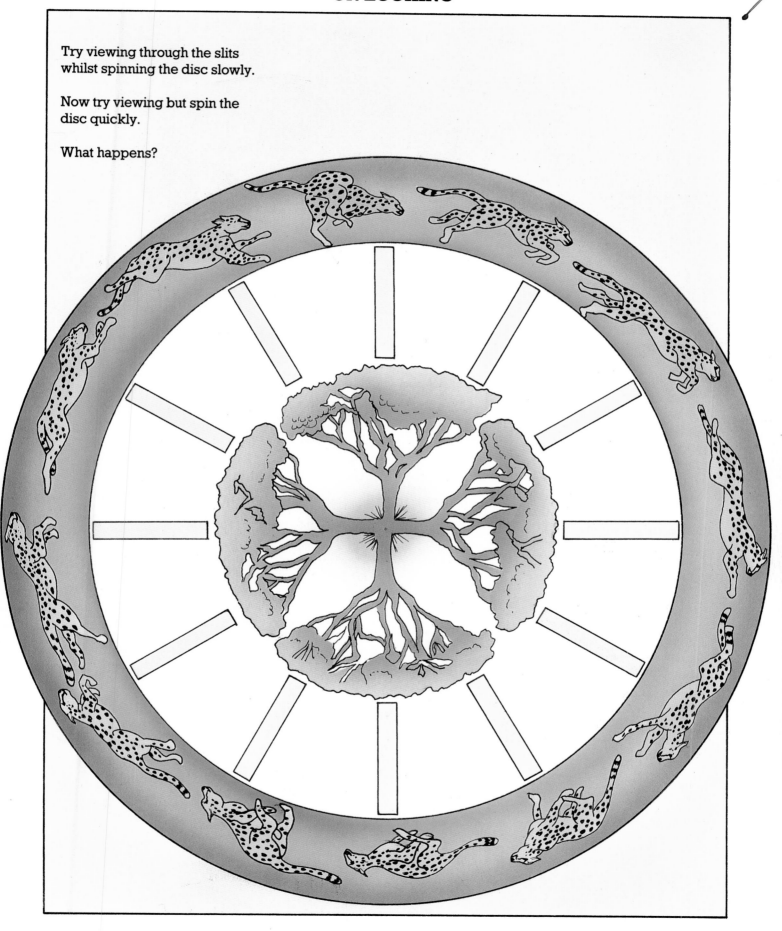

FLICK BOOKS

It is easy to make a moving action picture book. You need a story line like the one shown on the opposite page. It has 32 pictures. Copy the series of pictures shown on the opposite page onto thin card.

1 Cut out each picture. Punch two holes at the side.

2 Put them in numbered order, starting from the bottom up. Put picture number 1 on the bottom. Tie them with thin string. Bind with sticky tape.

3 Hold the book by the bound end and flick the pages from back to front with your other hand. You will see the pictures move. Make up some more books. There are some suggestions below for story lines. You make up the "in between" pictures. Keep the pictures to the right.

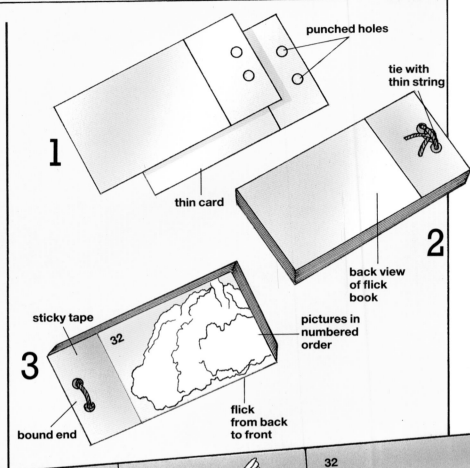

punched holes

tie with thin string

thin card

back view of flick book

pictures in numbered order

sticky tape

bound end

flick from back to front

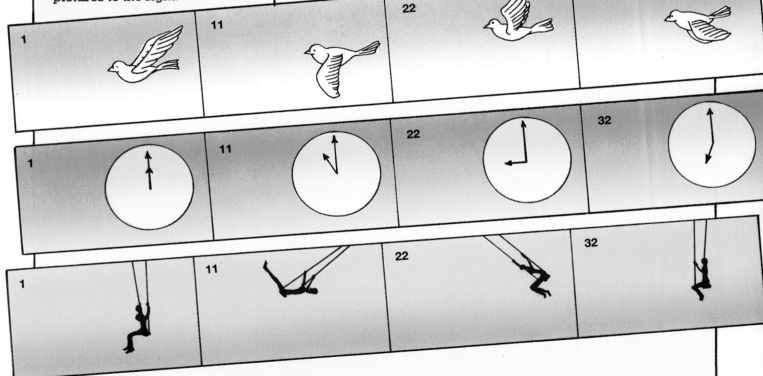

ZOETROPES

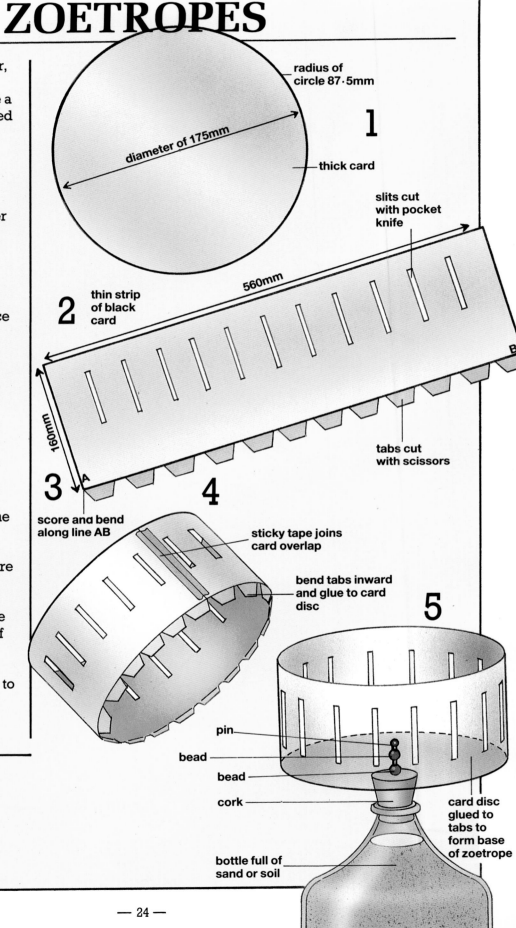

In 1834 William George Horner, an English mathematician, invented a device that became a popular Victorian toy. It enabled the Victorians to see moving pictures. You can make a zoetrope.

1 Draw a circle of radius 87·5 millimetres (diameter 175 millimetres) on thick card. Cut out the disc.

2 Cut a thin strip of black card 560 millimetres long and 160 millimetres wide. Trace the template on the opposite page and use it to give you the spacing for the slits and tabs. The slits must be cut out with a pocket Stanley knife. You can cut the tabs with scissors.

3 Score along line AB and bend the tabs inward.

4 Glue the tabs to the card disc. Join the overlap in the card with sticky tape.

5 Fix a pin through the centre of the zoetrope (with a bead either side so that it runs smoothly) into a cork. Stand the cork in a weighted bottle full of sand or soil.

You will need a strip of figures to stick inside your zoetrope. There are strips of figures for you to trace on page 25.

1 radius of circle 87·5mm

diameter of 175mm

thick card

2 thin strip of black card

560mm

slits cut with pocket knife

B

160mm

tabs cut with scissors

3 score and bend along line AB

A

4 sticky tape joins card overlap

bend tabs inward and glue to card disc

5 pin

bead

bead

cork

card disc glued to tabs to form base of zoetrope

bottle full of sand or soil

template for
tracing

1 Trace these figures below. Join AA to BB, CC to DD to make a continuous strip. Notice the movement is from right to left. Stick the strip in your zoetrope so that it runs round the edge of the drum just beneath the slits.

2 Spin the zoetrope. Peep through the slits. Can you see the figures moving? If you sit back from the zoetrope you will get a better picture.

3 There are two more strips for tracing opposite.

moving figures

stick strip

slits

zoetrope

figures for tracing

Join AA to BB, CC to DD

A

A

B

C

B

C

D

D

CURVES FROM CIRCLES

1 Take a pair of compasses and mark two points A and B, 100 millimetres apart.

2 Draw circles from each point. Increase the radius of each circle by 10 millimetres at a time.

3 Draw in ellipses as shown. Can you construct more?

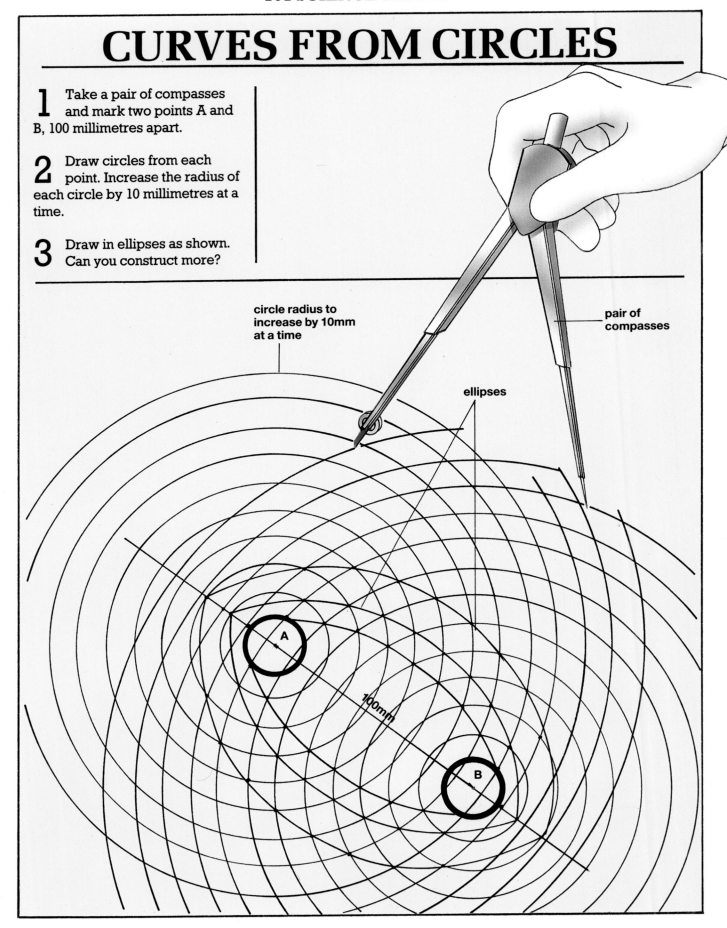

circle radius to increase by 10mm at a time

pair of compasses

ellipses

100mm

A

B

You can make all sorts of patterns. Here are two examples. The patterning shows the ellipses.

Try making other patterns by using different colours and choosing other parts of the design to colour in.

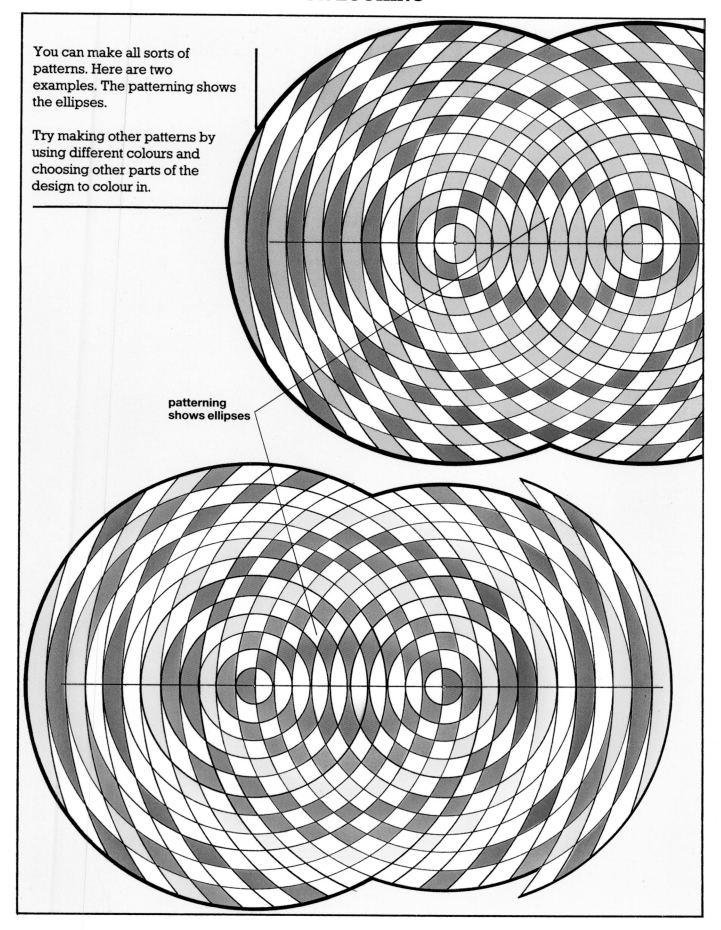

patterning shows ellipses

CIRCLES FROM LINES

1 Take a pair of compasses again and draw a circle. Mark every 10 degrees around the circle using a protractor. You will end up with 36 marks.

2 Draw a line across the circle connecting two marks, A B. Take the next set of marks, C, D and connect them. Notice C is below A and D is above B. Repeat the pattern all round the circle.

You will find that you make a new circle at the centre using your straight lines.

3 Draw a new line closer to the centre E F. Draw the next line G H, again with G below E and H above F. Continue as before.

You will now make a new circle at the centre.

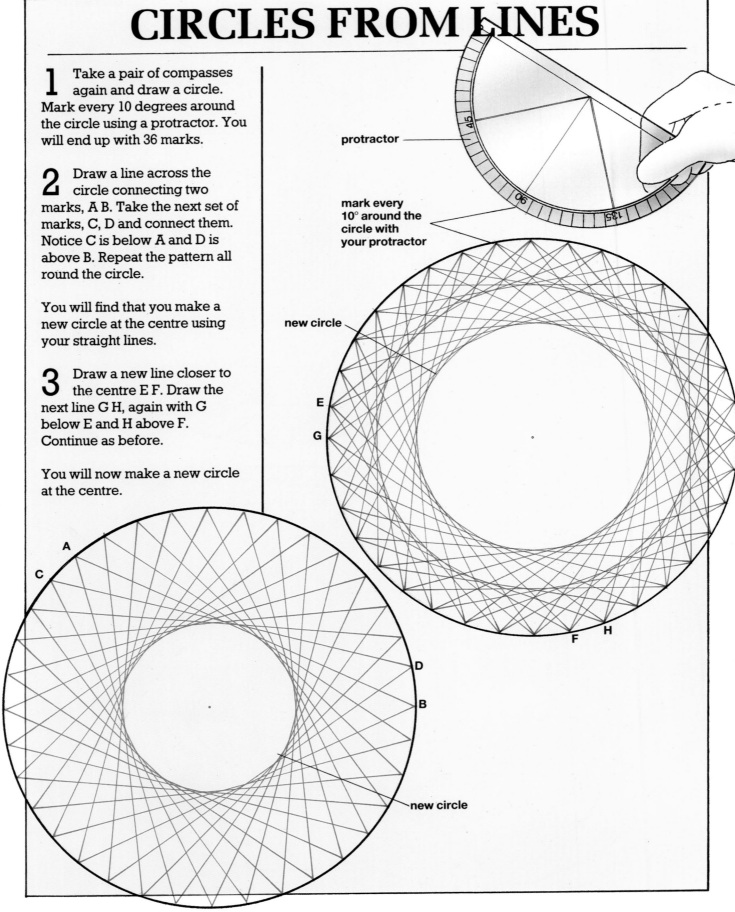

protractor

mark every 10° around the circle with your protractor

new circle

new circle

4 Draw a circle. Mark every 15 degrees around the circle using a protractor. You will end up with 24 marks. From every mark around the circle draw straight lines to every other mark. You will make the pattern below. It contains lots of new circles made from straight lines.

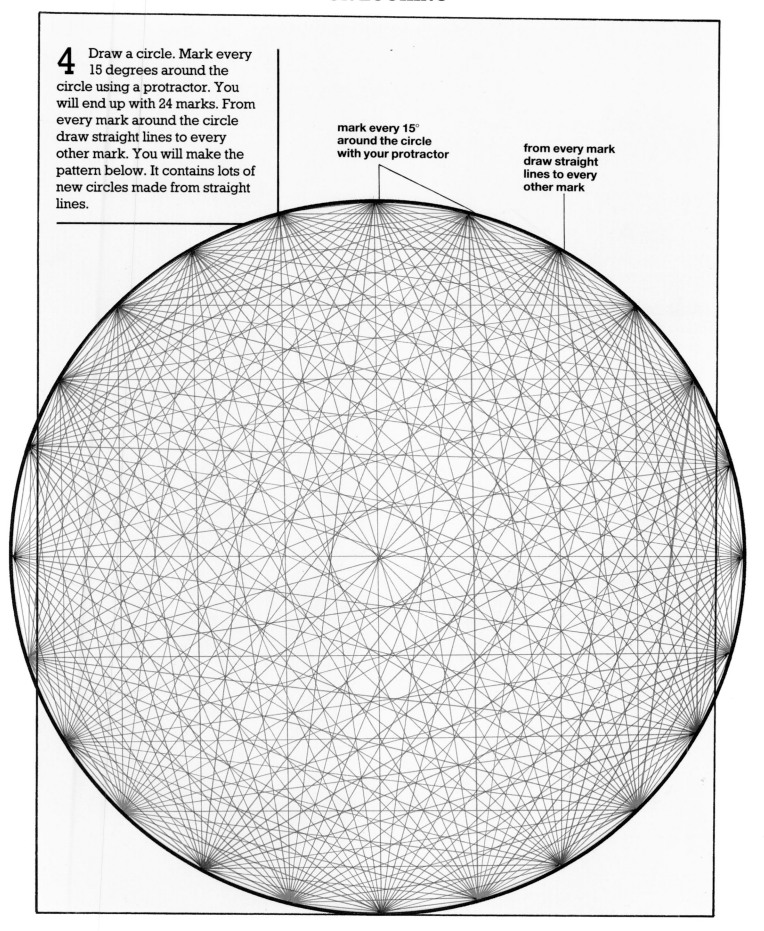

mark every 15°
around the circle
with your protractor

from every mark
draw straight
lines to every
other mark

MORE CURVES

A SINGLE CURVE

1 Draw an angle ABC. Mark off 5 millimetre sections on each line.

2 Draw lines DH, EI, FJ, GK and so on. You will find that you make a curve.

Try longer lines. Try changing the size of the angle.

A DOUBLE CURVE

Draw a circle. Use a protractor to mark every 5 degrees. You should have 72 marks. Draw lines AB, BD, CF, DH, EJ, and so on. Each line drawn is one mark beyond the previous starting mark and two marks on from the previous ending mark.

The result is a double curve.

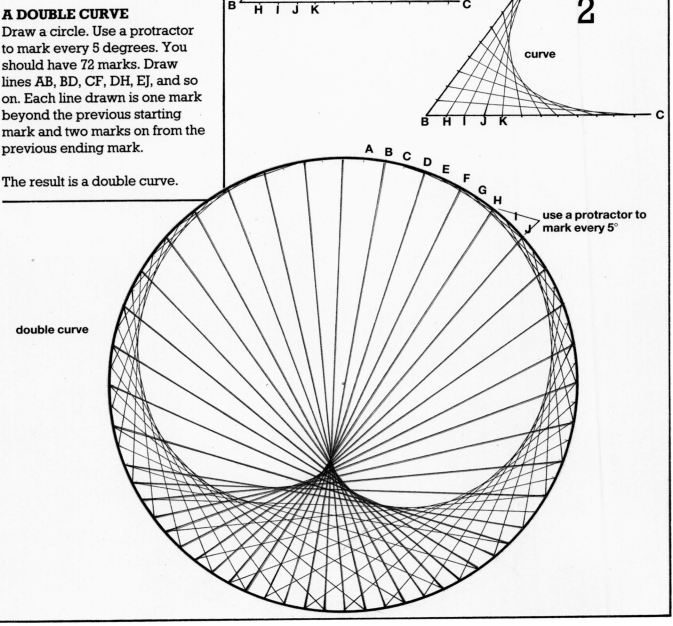

1 — angle ABC

5mm

2 — curve

use a protractor to mark every 5°

double curve

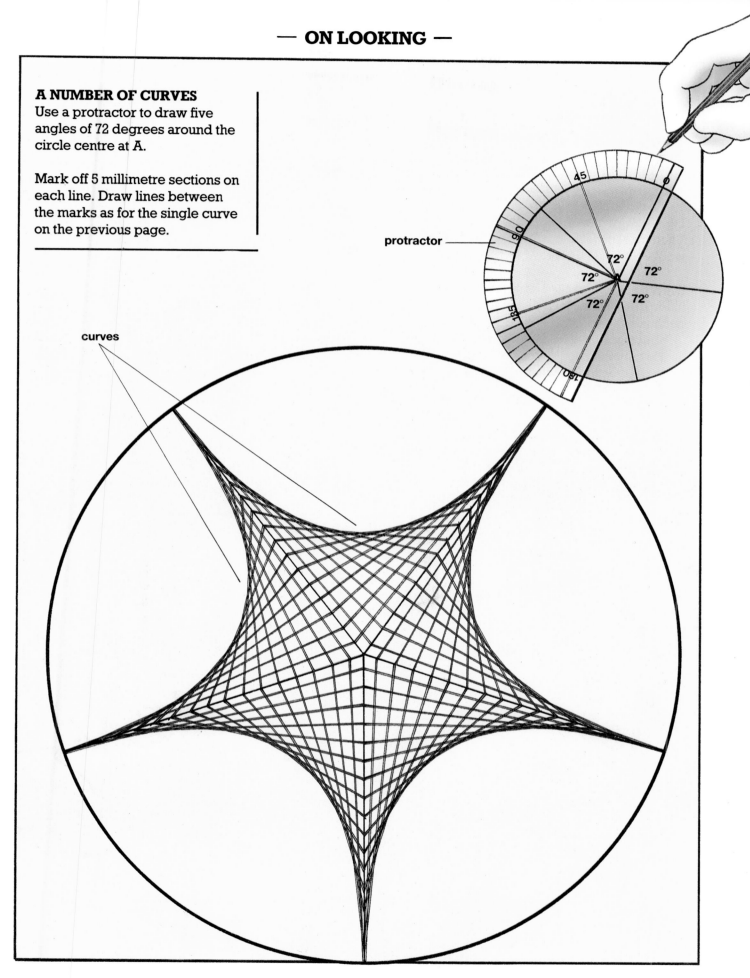

A NUMBER OF CURVES
Use a protractor to draw five angles of 72 degrees around the circle centre at A.

Mark off 5 millimetre sections on each line. Draw lines between the marks as for the single curve on the previous page.

protractor

curves

CURVE STITCHING

Using a needle or pins and darning wool many of the curved patterns that you have been drawing can be picked out on card to make a picture. Lightly draw your pattern first. Then make it using coloured wool.

Draw a square on card with 160 millimetre sides. Mark every 10 millimetres around the square. Connect these marks to make a single curve at each corner as described on the previous page.

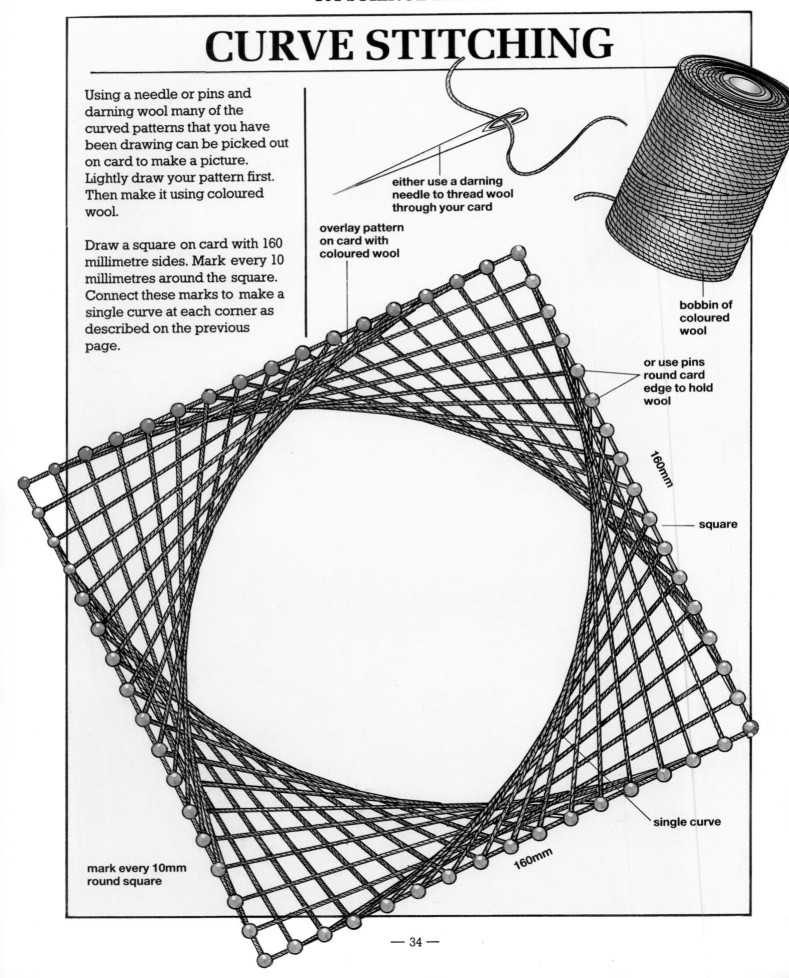

either use a darning needle to thread wool through your card

overlay pattern on card with coloured wool

bobbin of coloured wool

or use pins round card edge to hold wool

160mm

square

single curve

mark every 10mm round square

160mm

SPIRAL

Trace the spiral below onto card. Mark the 25 points. Join each point to the 24 others.

The pattern you get is the nautilus shell found in tropical waters. Look around for other spiral patterns. Garden snails, pine cones and spiral staircases are more examples.

Again, you could overlay the pattern with wool as shown in the picture on the right.

pattern of nautilus shell

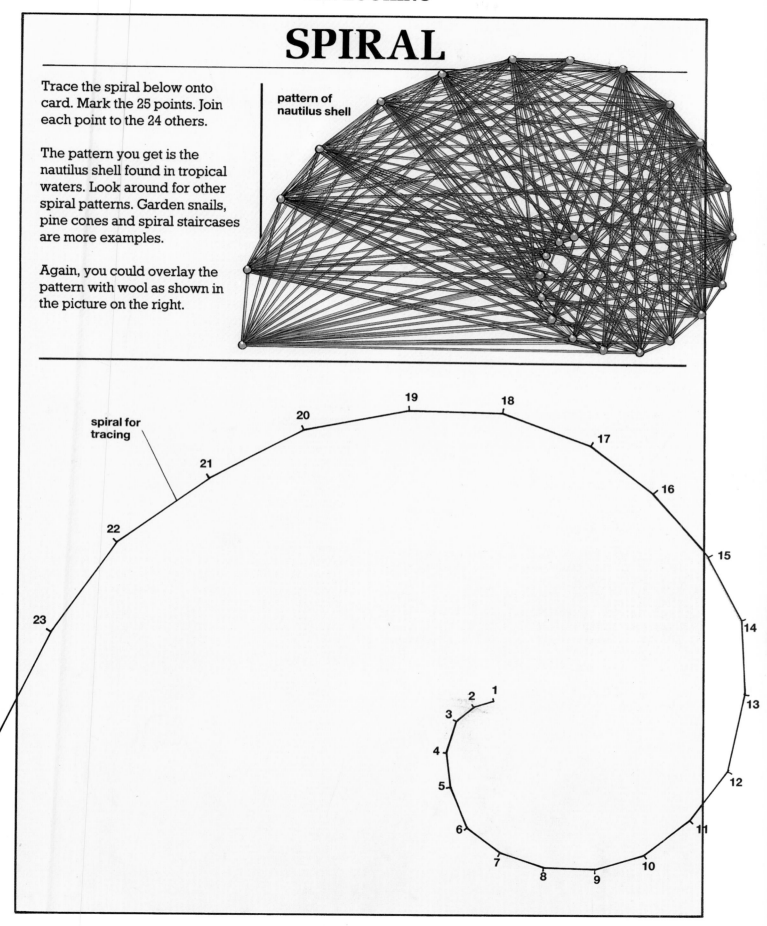

spiral for tracing

NOTES FOR PARENTS AND TEACHERS

Pages 7 – 27   These pages are concerned in some way or other with light and with the way we perceive things.

Children are learning that:
- light travels in straight lines
- light can be made to change direction
- shiny surfaces form images
- light can be reflected
- the brain can retain images to create an impression of movement.

All of these concepts are developed by carrying out the simple activities suggested. There is much that children can learn from investigations with mirrors.

Pages 7, 8 and 9   These are concerned with the way shiny mirror surfaces reflect well, and with reflective symmetry. They show how mirror images can be completed in both a horizontal and a vertical plane.

Pages 10 and 11   These show how putting two or more mirrors together can multiply the reflections and create a 'kaleidoscopic' effect.

Pages 12 and 13   These show how light can be bent through an angle of 90 degrees using a mirror and how this effect is put into use to produce a periscope.

Pages 14 and 15   Carrying out the activities on Page 14 results in each eye receiving a separate image. The brain merges these together so that we see one composite picture. Page 15 illustrates how visual images can deceive.

Pages 16 and 17   The brain can retain images for a short while. This ability is made use of in the spinning picture toy called the thaumatrope.

Pages 18 – 21   Again the ability of the brain to retain images for a short while is made use of in the phenakistoscope to give an impression of continuous movement.

Pages 22 – 23   The flick book reinforces the way we retain images, as we see a rapidly moving succession of pictures. This creates the illusion of movement.

Pages 24 – 27   This section completes the work on light and optical toys by showing how to make a zoetrope. The retention of images by the brain is made use of in a toy which was a precursor of modern cinema.

Pages 28 – 35   Here seeing is believing. We can use straight lines and circles to produce curves. This section is concerned with mathematical exploration. Children are learning that mathematics has pattern which is probably one of the most important things about mathematics.

They are learning that:
- straight lines can be used to produce circles
- chords drawn to a circle produce an inner circle called an envelope
- there are ellipses
- there is pattern in mathematics.

Pages 28 and 29   Introduce children to ellipses and pattern making.

Pages 30 and 31   Show how drawing chords to a circle produces an inner circle which mathematicians call an envelope.

Pages 32 and 33   Develop the idea of getting curves from straight lines.

Pages 34 and 35   Show how wool can be used to make a picture commonly known as curved stitching. On Page 35 children can find out how straight lines can be used to develop the idea of making a spiral.

2
on the
Move

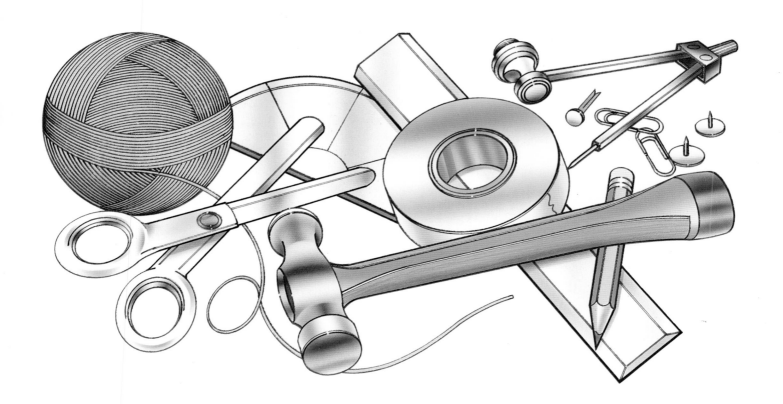

INTRODUCTION

Have you ever wondered what makes things move? What made the first boats, planes, rockets, and tanks move? In **On the Move** you will find that there are a lot of things to do and make. They will take you up in the air, along the ground and into the water and will enable you to see what makes things move. With a flick of the wrist your acrobatic plane will loop the loop, with a little bit of wind your kite will take to the skies; and with a few winds of the elastic band your cotton reel tank will start to crawl and your water-screw boat begin to speed. Find out how to make a paper windmill, a jumping Jack or a trotting mouse to give to your friends. Discover how to flick a boomerang, twirl a helicopter and spin a top. There is lots more to do and everything you need is listed on page 101.

PAPER PLANE

Take a sheet of A4 paper
(210 x 297 millimetres).

1 Fold the two opposite
corners together.

2 Fold the bottom edge up
half the distance of "x".

3 Fold the paper in half along
the dotted line.

4 Fold the bottom sections
upward.

5 Fold the wings down along
the dotted line.

6 Staple the nose
and tail.

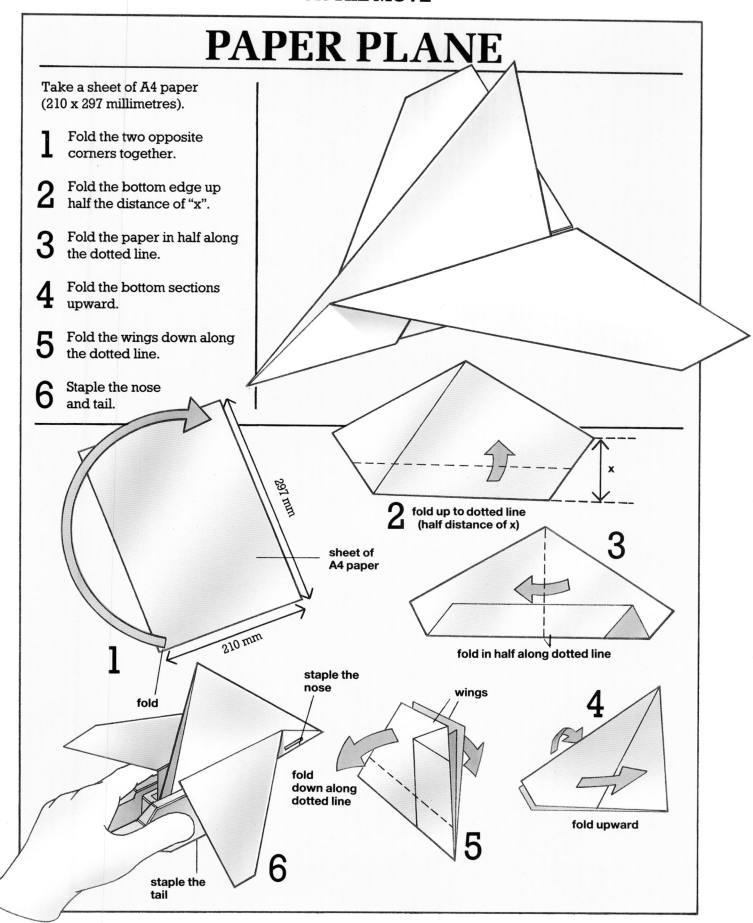

1 fold

297 mm

sheet of
A4 paper

210 mm

2 fold up to dotted line
(half distance of x)

x

3 fold in half along dotted line

4 fold upward

5 wings

fold
down along
dotted line

6 staple the
nose

staple the
tail

PAPER DART

Use one sheet of A4 paper to make a paper dart.

1 Fold in half.

2 Open out and fold the corner over.

3 Fold the other corner over.

4 Fold the paper again, like this.

5 Turn the other corner down.

6 Turn over.

7 Fold sides to centre.

8 Fold again.

9 Fold in half.

10 Hold the centre fold and open out.

11 Fix the paper dart with sticky tape.

12 Launch it.

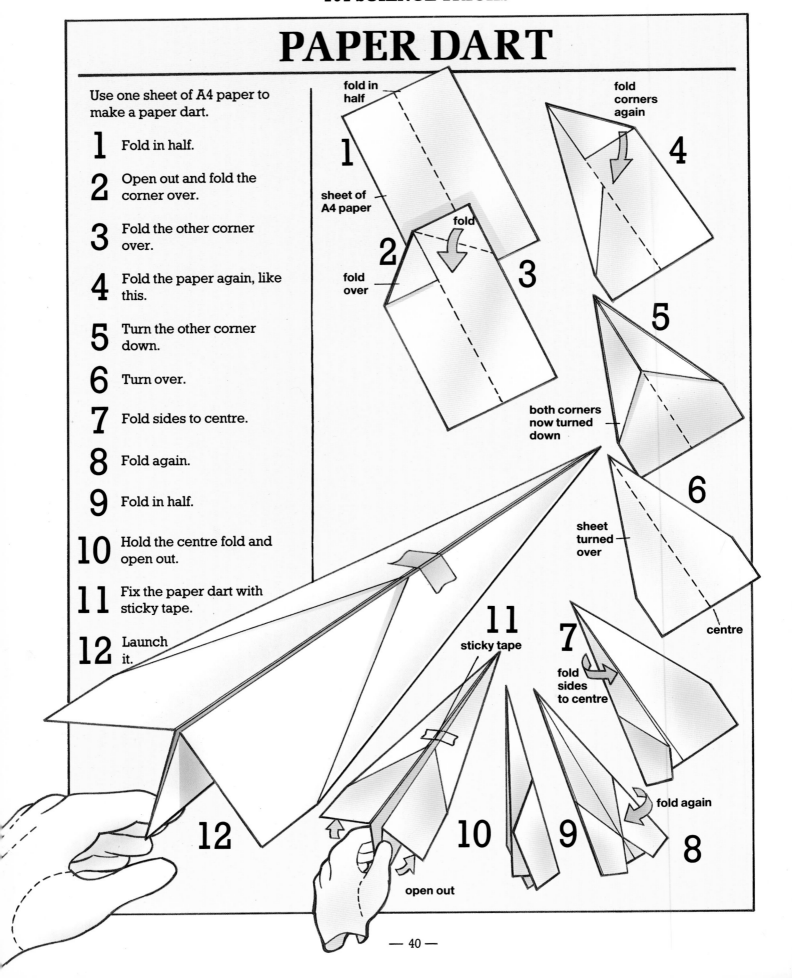

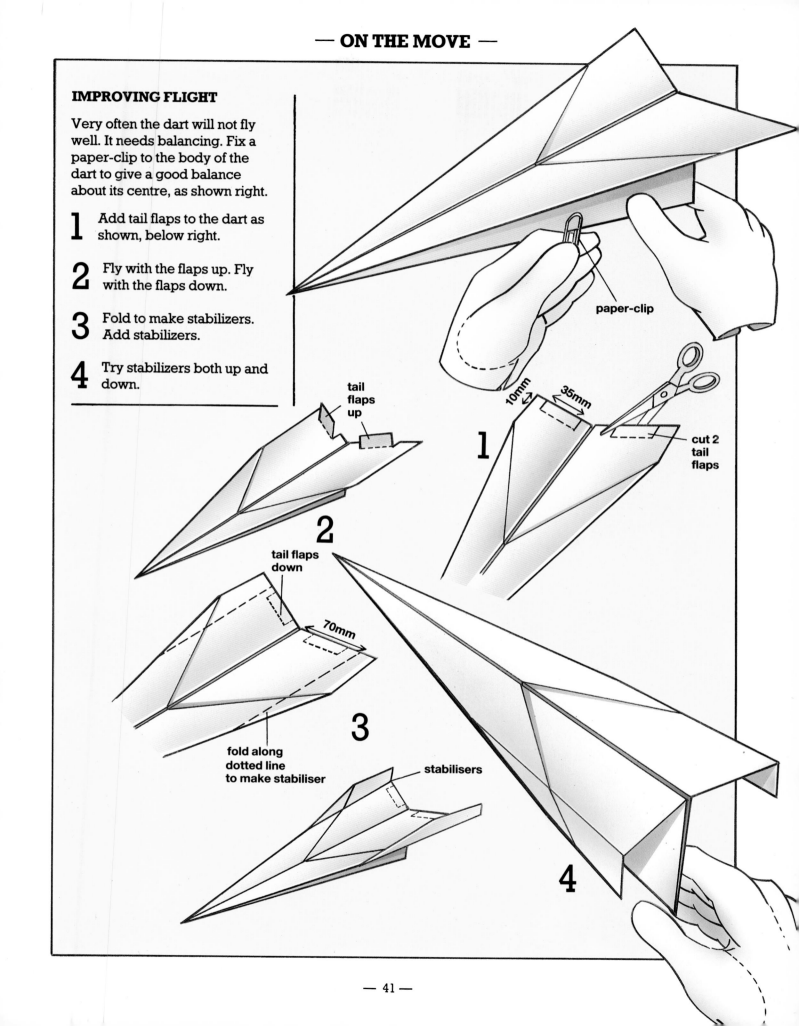

IMPROVING FLIGHT

Very often the dart will not fly well. It needs balancing. Fix a paper-clip to the body of the dart to give a good balance about its centre, as shown right.

1 Add tail flaps to the dart as shown, below right.

2 Fly with the flaps up. Fly with the flaps down.

3 Fold to make stabilizers. Add stabilizers.

4 Try stabilizers both up and down.

paper-clip

10mm   35mm

1   cut 2 tail flaps

tail flaps up

2

tail flaps down

70mm

3

fold along dotted line to make stabiliser

stabilisers

4

DELTA WING

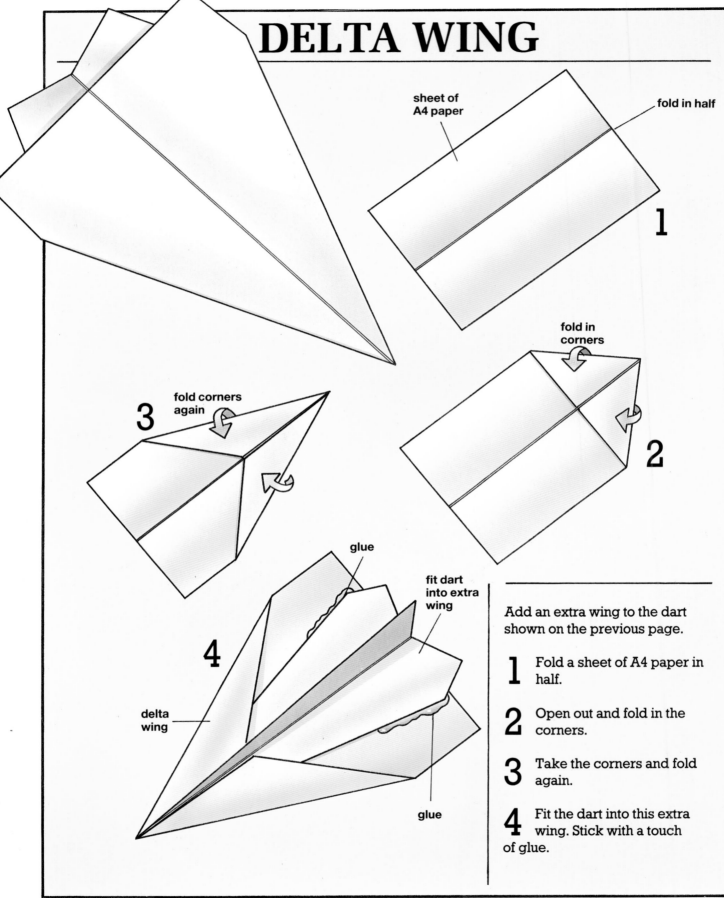

sheet of A4 paper

fold in half

1

fold in corners

2

fold corners again

3

glue

fit dart into extra wing

4

delta wing

glue

Add an extra wing to the dart shown on the previous page.

1 Fold a sheet of A4 paper in half.

2 Open out and fold in the corners.

3 Take the corners and fold again.

4 Fit the dart into this extra wing. Stick with a touch of glue.

ACROBATIC PLANE

1 Fold a sheet of A4 paper crosswise.

2 Open up and fold a crease 13 millimetres from the edge of the long side.

3 Fold and fold again several times.

4 Refold to centre line. Cut out a notch in the paper as below.

5 Open out the acrobatic plane.

6 Fold the wing tips of the plane up.

7 Fold down the outer edges of the tail.

8 Check the plane for symmetry. It is essential that one half is a mirror image of the other.

9 Launch the plane gently away from you with a slight downward motion.

TIPS

1 If the plane glides all right but moves from side to side check the symmetry.

2 If the plane dives turn the trailing edge of the tail up a little.

3 If the plane undulates turn the trailing edges of the tail down. If this is not successful the plane may be too heavy in the tail. Try a tiny piece of Plasticine or a paper-clip on the nose.

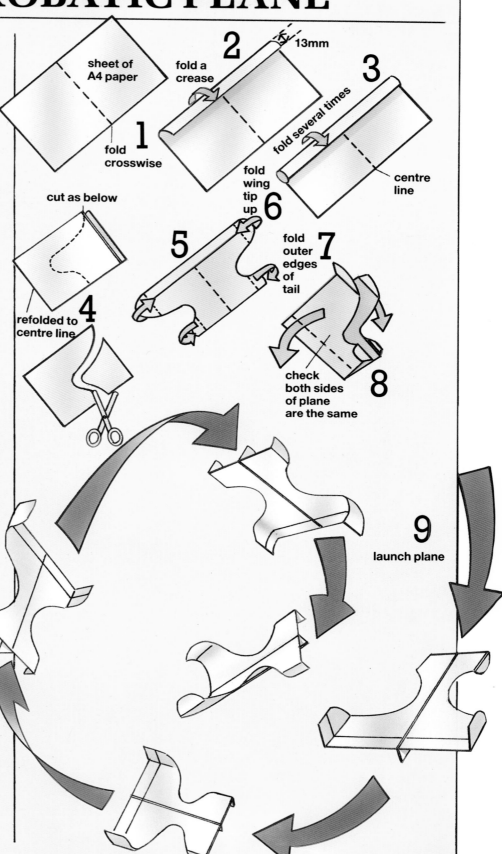

1 sheet of A4 paper — fold crosswise

2 fold a crease — 13mm

3 fold several times — centre line

4 cut as below — refolded to centre line

5 fold wing tip up

6 fold wing tip up

7 fold outer edges of tail

8 check both sides of plane are the same

9 launch plane

BALSA WOOD GLIDER

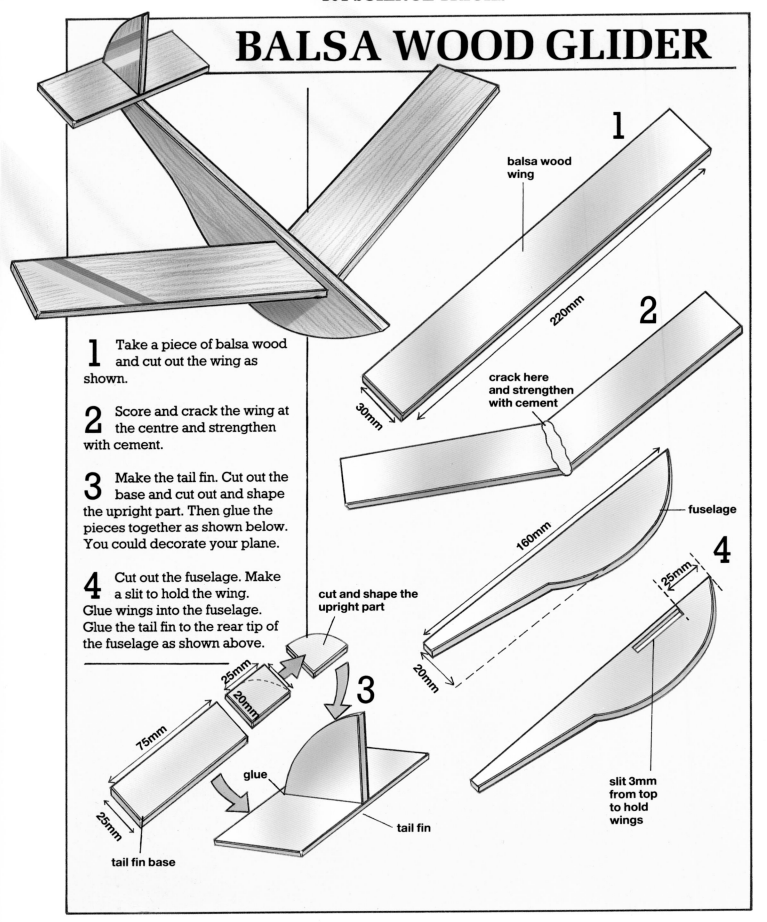

balsa wood wing

1

220mm

30mm

2

crack here and strengthen with cement

fuselage

160mm

20mm

4

25mm

slit 3mm from top to hold wings

1 Take a piece of balsa wood and cut out the wing as shown.

2 Score and crack the wing at the centre and strengthen with cement.

3 Make the tail fin. Cut out the base and cut out and shape the upright part. Then glue the pieces together as shown below. You could decorate your plane.

4 Cut out the fuselage. Make a slit to hold the wing. Glue wings into the fuselage. Glue the tail fin to the rear tip of the fuselage as shown above.

cut and shape the upright part

3

25mm

20mm

75mm

25mm

glue

tail fin

tail fin base

JET ROCKET

This balloon rocket runs on nylon fishing line fixed tightly across a room.

1 Thread two short pieces of drinking straw onto the line.

2 Blow up the balloon. Close the neck of the balloon with a bulldog clip.

3 Tape the straws to the inflated balloon with sticky tape. Make sure the fishing line is taut and straight.

4 When you are ready to launch your rocket, remove the clip to release the balloon.

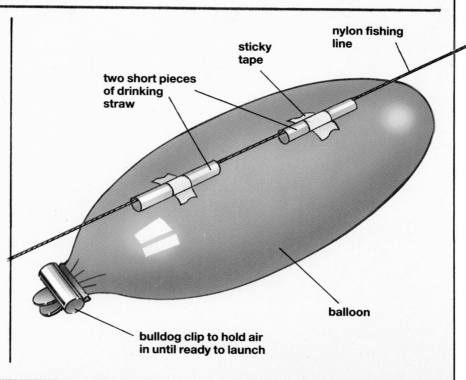

nylon fishing line

sticky tape

two short pieces of drinking straw

balloon

bulldog clip to hold air in until ready to launch

PROPELLER-DRIVEN PLANE

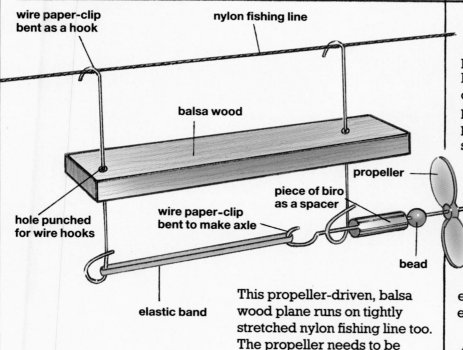

wire paper-clip bent as a hook

nylon fishing line

balsa wood

hole punched for wire hooks

wire paper-clip bent to make axle

piece of biro as a spacer

propeller

bead

elastic band

This propeller-driven, balsa wood plane runs on tightly stretched nylon fishing line too. The propeller needs to be bought from a hobby shop.

1 Use a wire paper-clip to make the axle to hold the propeller. You need a bead to help it run smoothly and a piece of Biro as a spacer. Thread the piece of Biro and the bead and propeller onto your wire axle as shown.

2 Bend two other paper-clips to make the wire hooks that pass through the balsa wood body of the plane.

3 Wind the propeller round and round to twist the elastic band and give the plane elastic energy.

4 Release the propeller and watch the plane whizz along.

PARACHUTES

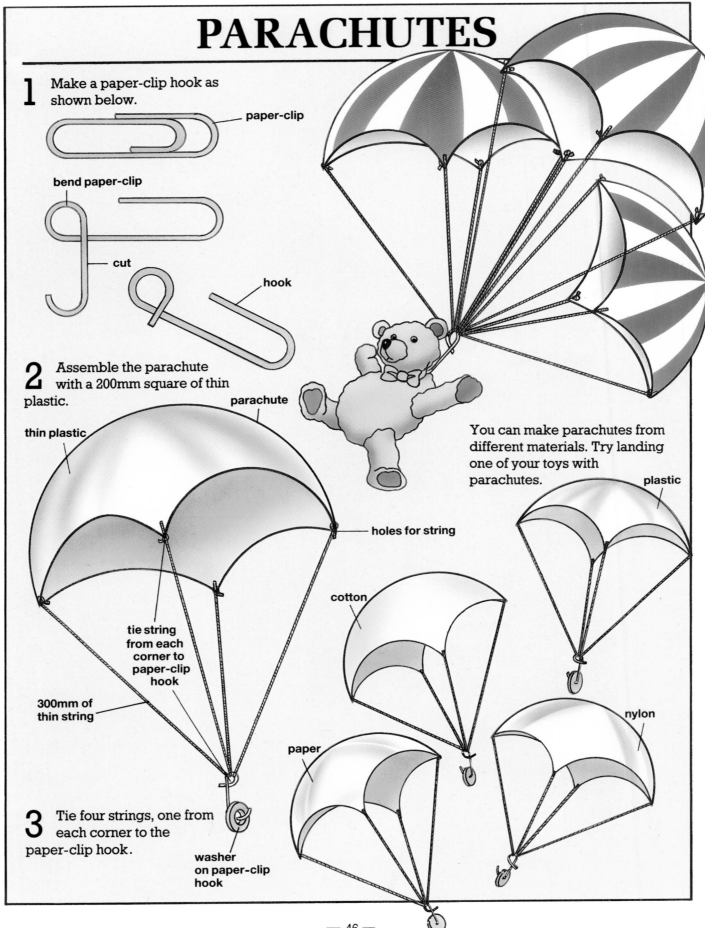

1 Make a paper-clip hook as shown below.

paper-clip

bend paper-clip

cut

hook

2 Assemble the parachute with a 200mm square of thin plastic.

thin plastic

parachute

holes for string

tie string from each corner to paper-clip hook

300mm of thin string

You can make parachutes from different materials. Try landing one of your toys with parachutes.

plastic

cotton

nylon

paper

3 Tie four strings, one from each corner to the paper-clip hook.

washer on paper-clip hook

PAPER SPINNERS

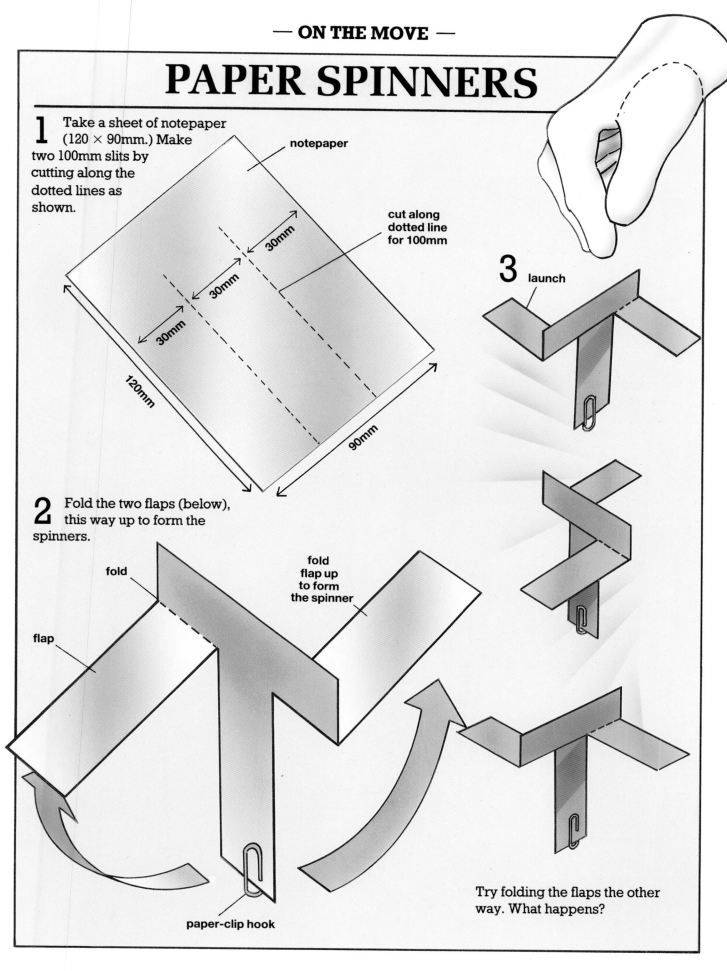

1 Take a sheet of notepaper (120 × 90mm.) Make two 100mm slits by cutting along the dotted lines as shown.

notepaper

cut along dotted line for 100mm

30mm

30mm

30mm

120mm

90mm

2 Fold the two flaps (below), this way up to form the spinners.

fold

flap

fold flap up to form the spinner

paper-clip hook

3 launch

Try folding the flaps the other way. What happens?

BOOMERANGS

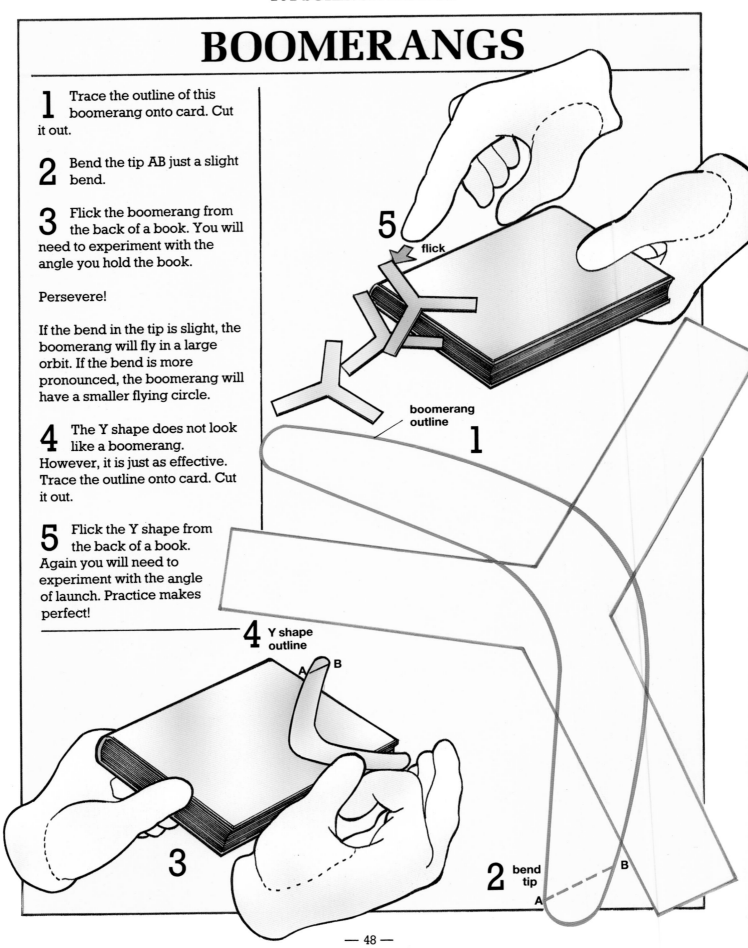

1 Trace the outline of this boomerang onto card. Cut it out.

2 Bend the tip AB just a slight bend.

3 Flick the boomerang from the back of a book. You will need to experiment with the angle you hold the book.

Persevere!

If the bend in the tip is slight, the boomerang will fly in a large orbit. If the bend is more pronounced, the boomerang will have a smaller flying circle.

4 The Y shape does not look like a boomerang. However, it is just as effective. Trace the outline onto card. Cut it out.

5 Flick the Y shape from the back of a book. Again you will need to experiment with the angle of launch. Practice makes perfect!

5 flick

boomerang outline

1

4 Y shape outline

A B

3

2 bend tip

A B

WINDMILLS

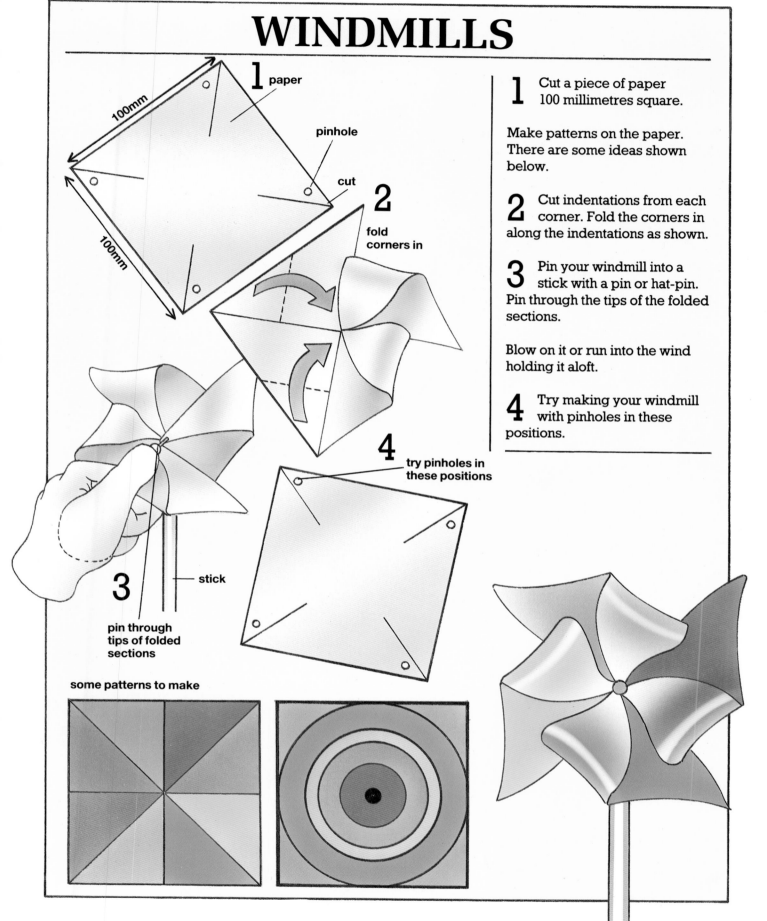

1 **paper**

100mm

pinhole

100mm

cut

2

fold corners in

3

stick

pin through tips of folded sections

4 **try pinholes in these positions**

some patterns to make

1 Cut a piece of paper 100 millimetres square.

Make patterns on the paper. There are some ideas shown below.

2 Cut indentations from each corner. Fold the corners in along the indentations as shown.

3 Pin your windmill into a stick with a pin or hat-pin. Pin through the tips of the folded sections.

Blow on it or run into the wind holding it aloft.

4 Try making your windmill with pinholes in these positions.

TIN HELICOPTER

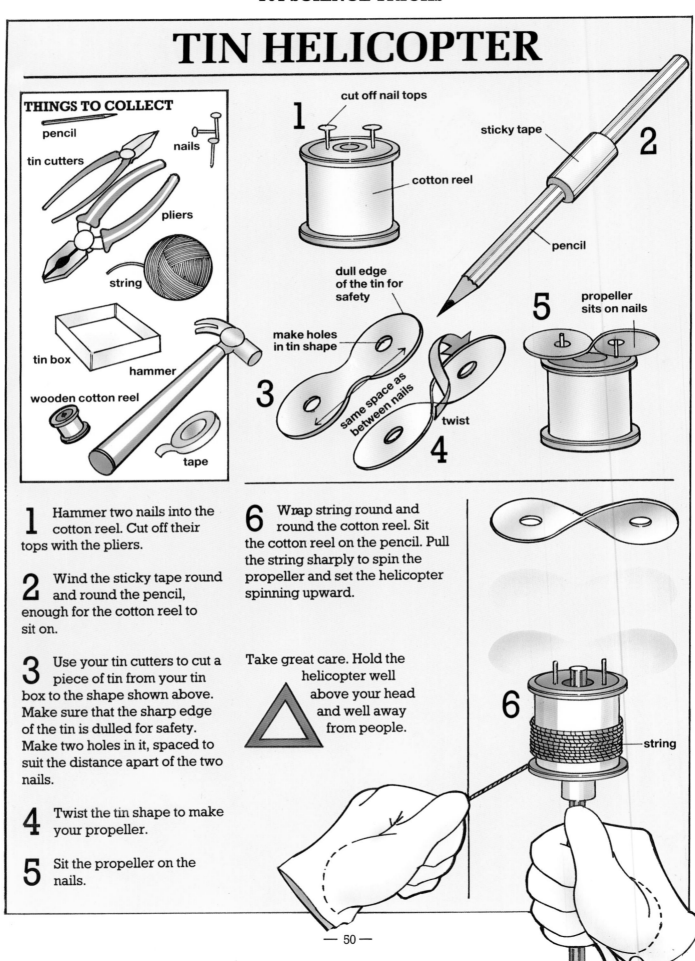

THINGS TO COLLECT

pencil

nails

tin cutters

pliers

string

tin box

hammer

wooden cotton reel

tape

1 cut off nail tops

cotton reel

2 sticky tape

pencil

3 dull edge of the tin for safety

make holes in tin shape

same space as between nails

twist

4

5 propeller sits on nails

1 Hammer two nails into the cotton reel. Cut off their tops with the pliers.

2 Wind the sticky tape round and round the pencil, enough for the cotton reel to sit on.

3 Use your tin cutters to cut a piece of tin from your tin box to the shape shown above. Make sure that the sharp edge of the tin is dulled for safety. Make two holes in it, spaced to suit the distance apart of the two nails.

4 Twist the tin shape to make your propeller.

5 Sit the propeller on the nails.

6 Wrap string round and round the cotton reel. Sit the cotton reel on the pencil. Pull the string sharply to spin the propeller and set the helicopter spinning upward.

Take great care. Hold the helicopter well above your head and well away from people.

6 string

PLASTIC HELICOPTER

Take any flat-sided plastic container.

1 Use a pair of scissors to cut a strip of plastic from this flat-sided container.

2 Make a hole through the centre of the plastic strip with a nail.

3 Push a pencil through the plastic. Twist the plastic strip slightly to make your helicopter.

4 Spin the helicopter in your hand and throw it into the air.

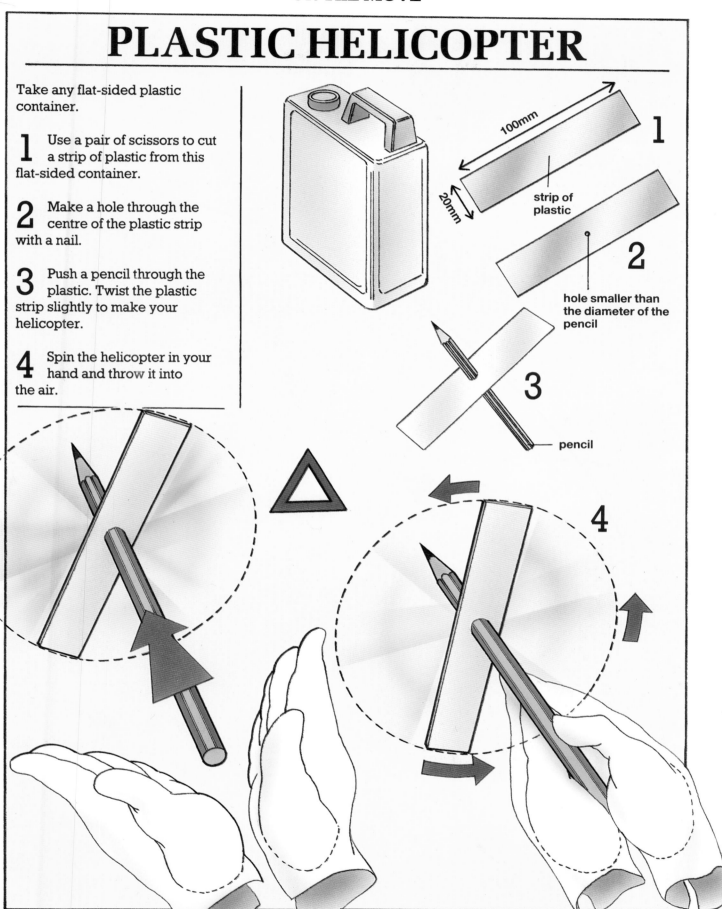

100mm

20mm

strip of plastic

1

2

hole smaller than the diameter of the pencil

3

pencil

4

KITE

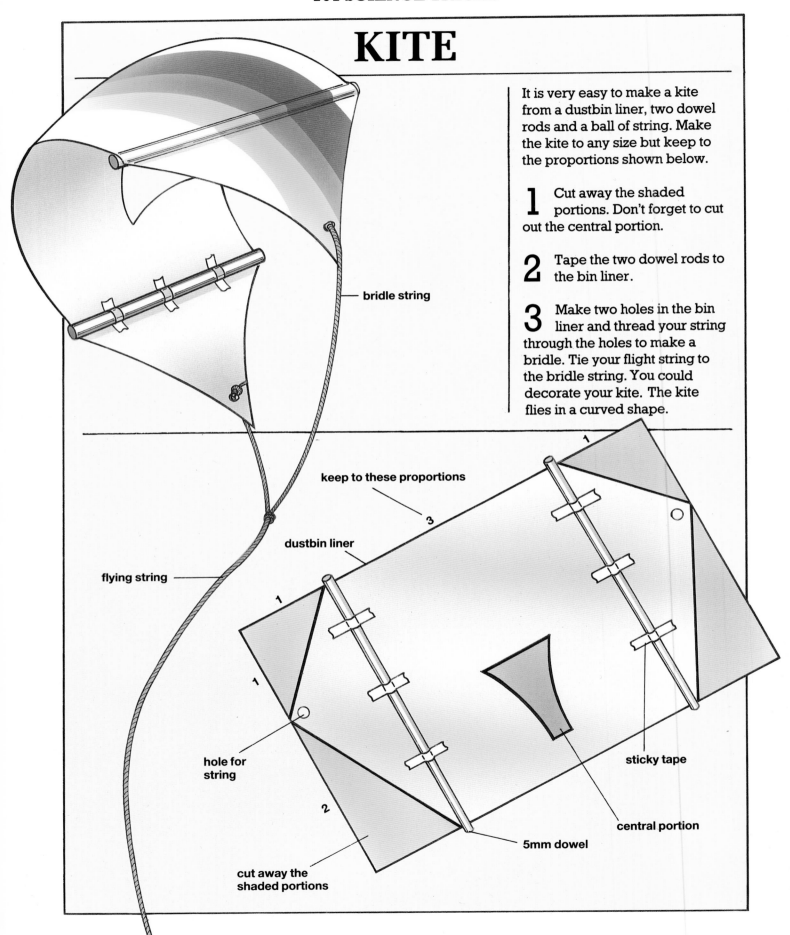

It is very easy to make a kite from a dustbin liner, two dowel rods and a ball of string. Make the kite to any size but keep to the proportions shown below.

1 Cut away the shaded portions. Don't forget to cut out the central portion.

2 Tape the two dowel rods to the bin liner.

3 Make two holes in the bin liner and thread your string through the holes to make a bridle. Tie your flight string to the bridle string. You could decorate your kite. The kite flies in a curved shape.

bridle string

keep to these proportions

dustbin liner

flying string

hole for string

sticky tape

central portion

5mm dowel

cut away the shaded portions

HOT-AIR BALLOON

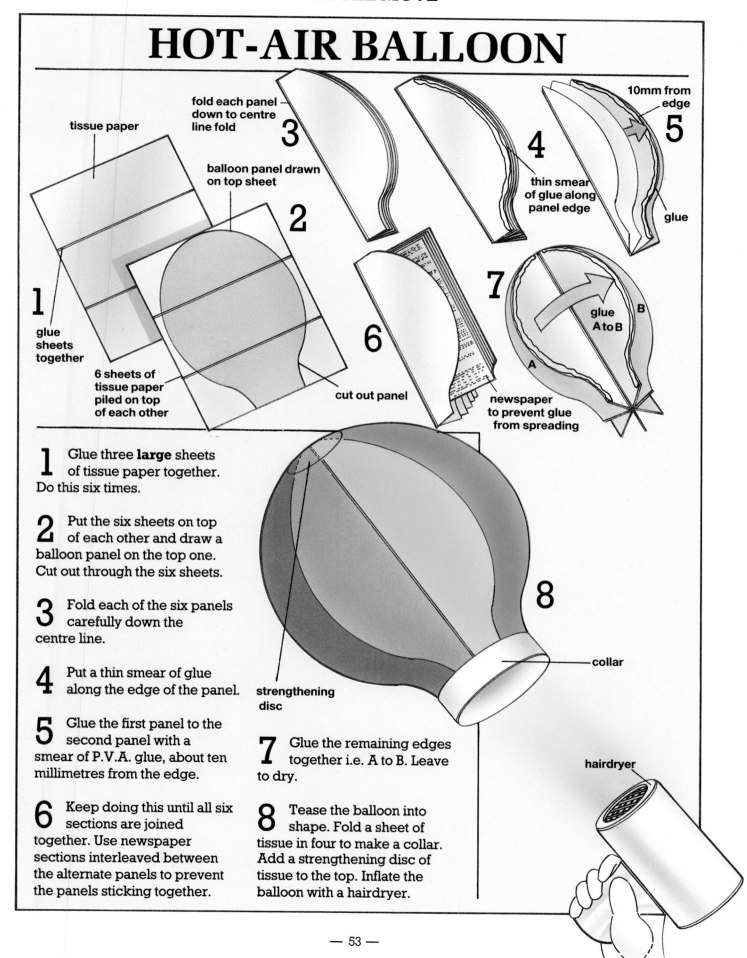

tissue paper

fold each panel down to centre line fold

3

4

thin smear of glue along panel edge

10mm from edge

5

glue

balloon panel drawn on top sheet

2

1

glue sheets together

6 sheets of tissue paper piled on top of each other

6

cut out panel

7

glue A to B

A

B

newspaper to prevent glue from spreading

strengthening disc

8

collar

hairdryer

1 Glue three **large** sheets of tissue paper together. Do this six times.

2 Put the six sheets on top of each other and draw a balloon panel on the top one. Cut out through the six sheets.

3 Fold each of the six panels carefully down the centre line.

4 Put a thin smear of glue along the edge of the panel.

5 Glue the first panel to the second panel with a smear of P.V.A. glue, about ten millimetres from the edge.

6 Keep doing this until all six sections are joined together. Use newspaper sections interleaved between the alternate panels to prevent the panels sticking together.

7 Glue the remaining edges together i.e. A to B. Leave to dry.

8 Tease the balloon into shape. Fold a sheet of tissue in four to make a collar. Add a strengthening disc of tissue to the top. Inflate the balloon with a hairdryer.

COTTON-REEL TANK

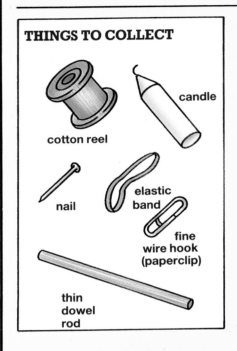
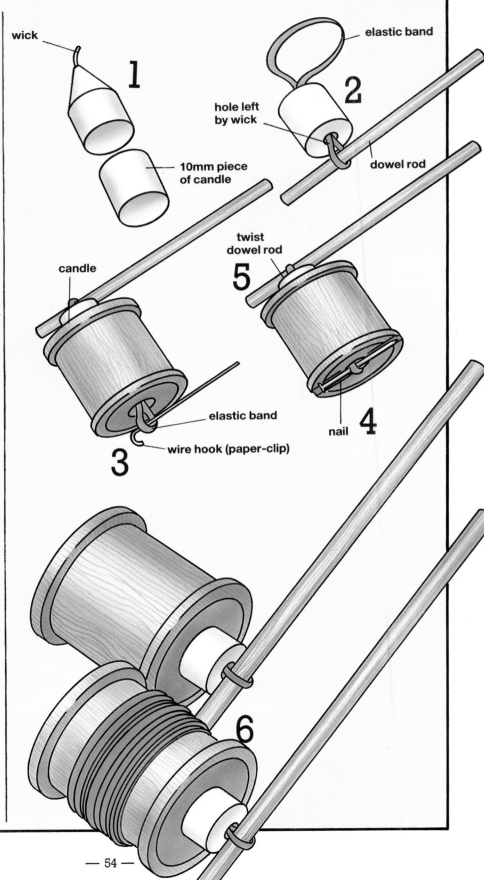

wick

1

10mm piece of candle

elastic band

2

hole left by wick

dowel rod

candle

5

twist dowel rod

3

elastic band

wire hook (paper-clip)

nail

4

6

1   Cut a 10 millimetre piece off the candle. You may need to ask a parent or teacher to cut the candle for you.

2   Make a hole through the centre of the candle by pulling out the wick. Thread the elastic band through the candle and secure it with the dowel.

3   Pull the free end of the elastic band through the cotton reel with the wire hook.

4   Secure the free end of the elastic band with a nail.

5   Wind the elastic by twisting the dowel rod round and round. Place the cotton reel tank on the ground and watch it move.

6   Wind with elastic band to help the tank grip when climbing slopes.

DRINK CAN DRAGSTER

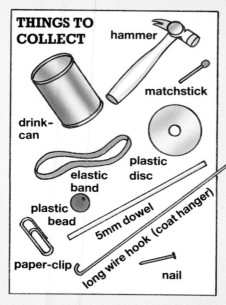

THINGS TO COLLECT

hammer

matchstick

drink-can

plastic disc

elastic band

plastic bead

5mm dowel

paper-clip

long wire hook (coat hanger)

nail

1 Make a hole through the blank end of the can with a nail.

2 Straighten out the paper-clip to make a hook.

3 Put the hook through the disc and the plastic bead.

4 Bend the straight end of the wire on the dowel rod and twist it around.

5 Use the long wire hook to pull an elastic band through the can.

6 Secure the other end of the elastic band to a matchstick.

7 Wind the rod round and round so that the elastic winds tightly and then release the dragster.

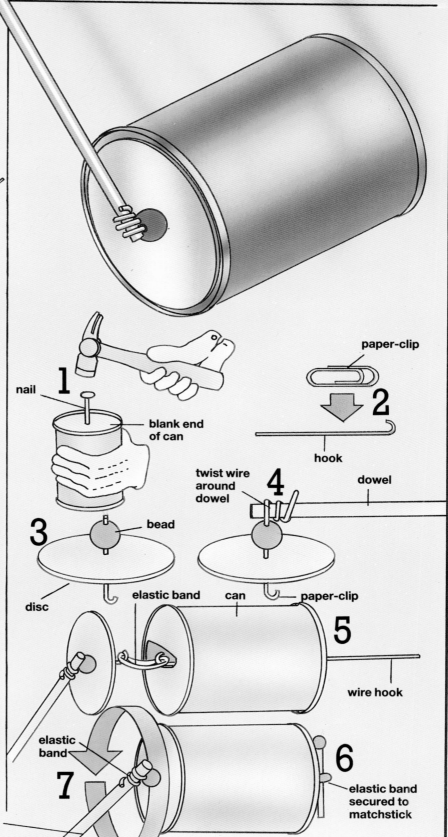

paper-clip

nail

1

blank end of can

2

hook

twist wire around dowel

4

dowel

3

bead

disc

elastic band

can

paper-clip

5

wire hook

elastic band

7

6

elastic band secured to matchstick

dowel rod

LAND YACHT

THINGS TO COLLECT

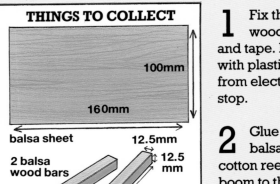

balsa sheet — 100mm × 160mm

2 balsa wood bars — 12.5mm / 12.5 mm / 100mm

4 model plane wheels

reel

peg

two thin dowel rods

plastic covered wire

tape

dustbin liner

1 Fix the wheels to the balsa wood bars with axle wire and tape. Hold the wheels on with plastic insulation stripped from electrical wire to act as a stop.

2 Glue the balsa sheet to the balsa bars. Glue on the cotton reel. Fix the dowel rod boom to the clothes peg with the elastic bands. Put the dowel rod mast into the centre of the cotton reel. Fix the boom to the mast with the clothes peg.

3 Cut and fix a piece of bin liner as a sail. You could use other material if you wish. Decorate your sail. Try your land yacht on a hard flat surface when there is some wind.

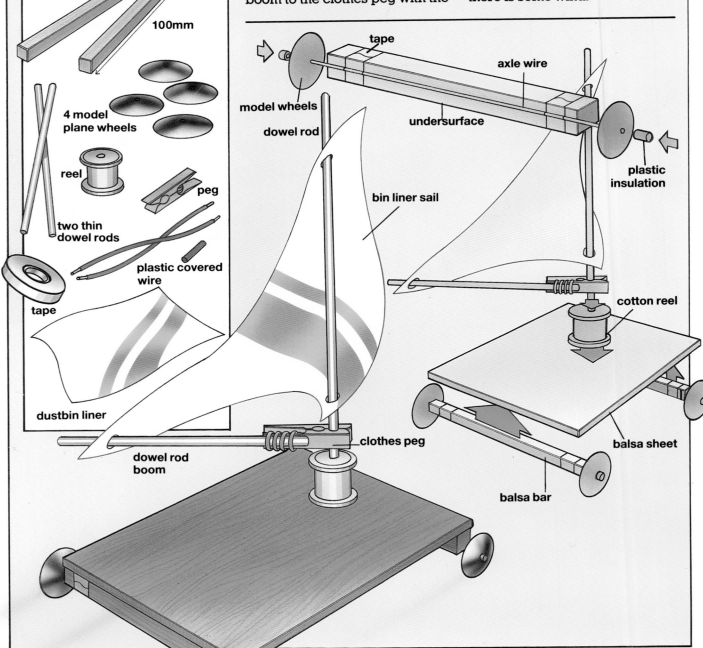

tape

axle wire

model wheels

dowel rod

undersurface

plastic insulation

bin liner sail

cotton reel

clothes peg

balsa sheet

dowel rod boom

balsa bar

TROLLEY

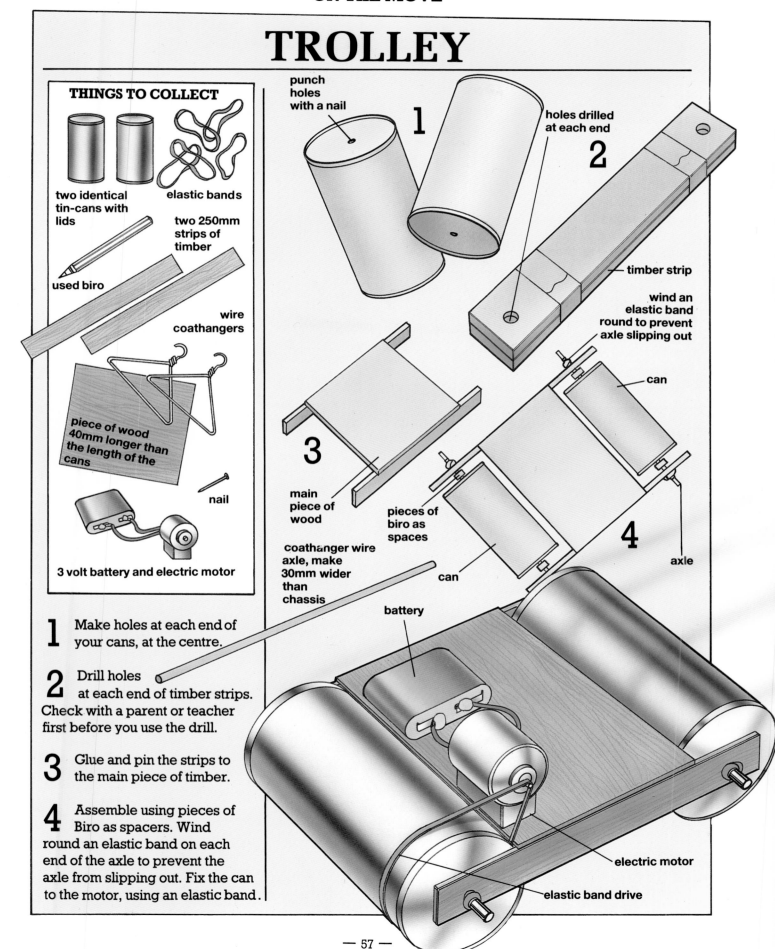

THINGS TO COLLECT

two identical tin-cans with lids

elastic bands

used biro

two 250mm strips of timber

wire coathangers

piece of wood 40mm longer than the length of the cans

nail

3 volt battery and electric motor

punch holes with a nail

1

holes drilled at each end

2

timber strip

wind an elastic band round to prevent axle slipping out

can

3

main piece of wood

pieces of biro as spaces

coathanger wire axle, make 30mm wider than chassis

can

4

axle

battery

electric motor

elastic band drive

1 Make holes at each end of your cans, at the centre.

2 Drill holes at each end of timber strips. Check with a parent or teacher first before you use the drill.

3 Glue and pin the strips to the main piece of timber.

4 Assemble using pieces of Biro as spacers. Wind round an elastic band on each end of the axle to prevent the axle from slipping out. Fix the can to the motor, using an elastic band.

JUMPING JACK

1 Trace these pieces of the Jack's body, (below), onto card. Cut them out and decorate them.

2 Fix the arms and legs to the main body with paper fasteners. Make small holes in the arms, legs and main body with the point of a Biro, and attach the string as shown.

3 Make a small hole in the Jack's head and attach the string to the head as shown. Hold the Jack by the string from the head. Pull the lower string to make him jump.

2

paper fasteners

small holes for string

3

string

1

arms

outline of main body

legs

cut shapes from card

MOUSE ON THE MOVE

1 Trace the legs and body of the mouse onto card.

2 Cut the shapes out and colour them in.

3 Fix the legs to the mouse with a paper fastener. Make sure the legs spin freely.

4 Fix a balsa rod to the mouse with glue. Use it to trundle the mouse along.

5 Stick string to the mouse's bottom to make a tail.

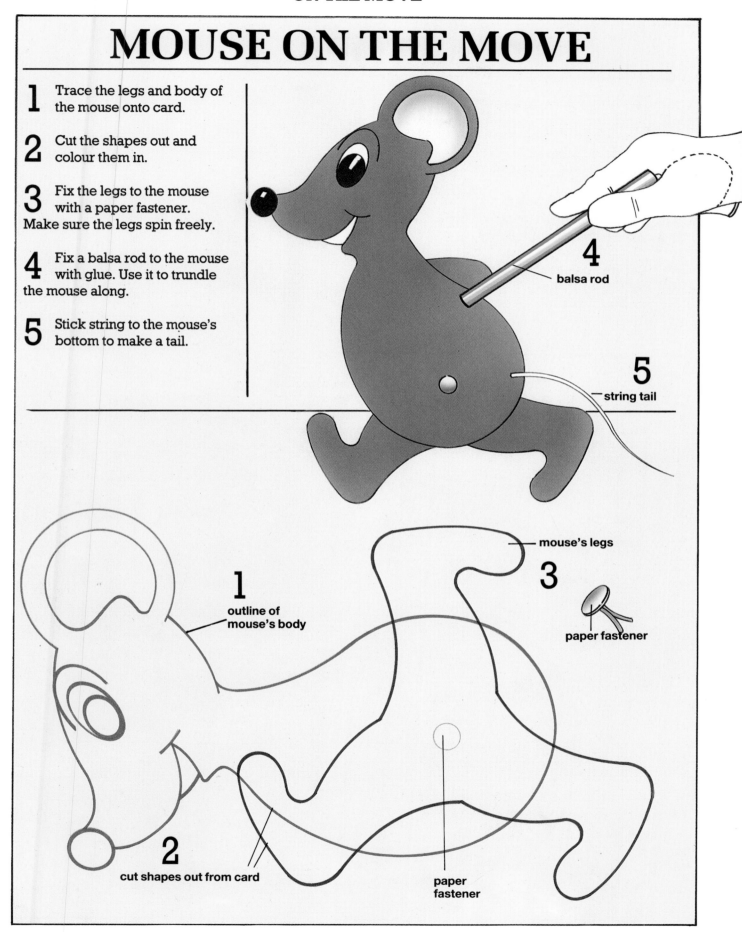

4 balsa rod

5 string tail

1 outline of mouse's body

2 cut shapes out from card

3 paper fastener

mouse's legs

paper fastener

TOPS

Make some tops from card.

1 Take a pair of compasses and draw some circles about 80 millimetres in diameter.

2 Decorate these circles. Make up different designs and coloured patterns as shown.

3 Cut your coloured circles out. Push a piece of dowel rod or a pencil through the centre of each circle to act as a spindle.

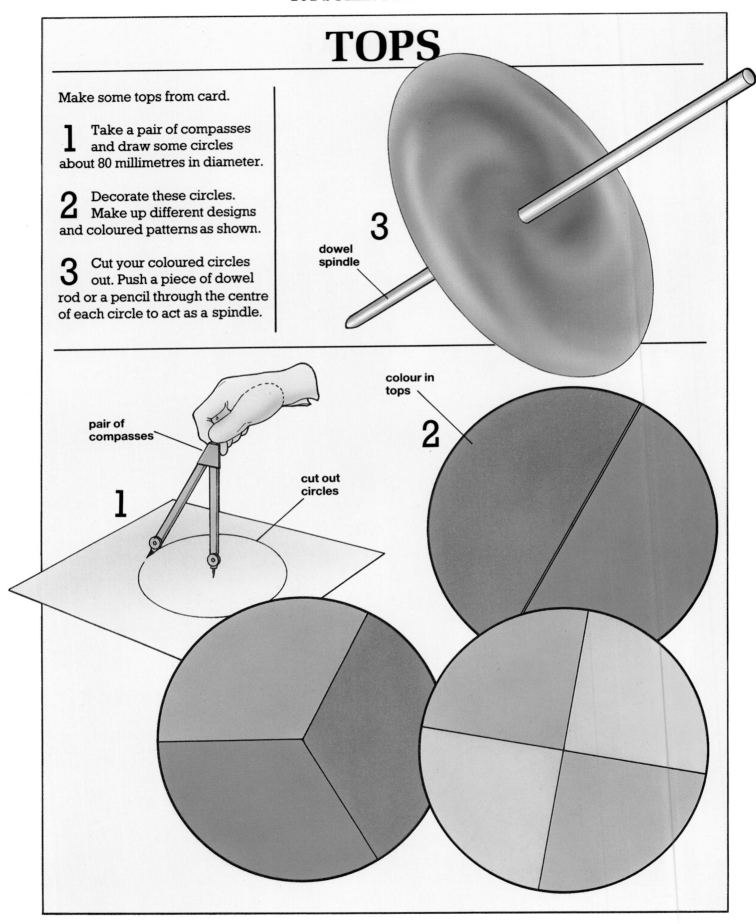

3

dowel spindle

colour in tops

2

pair of compasses

1

cut out circles

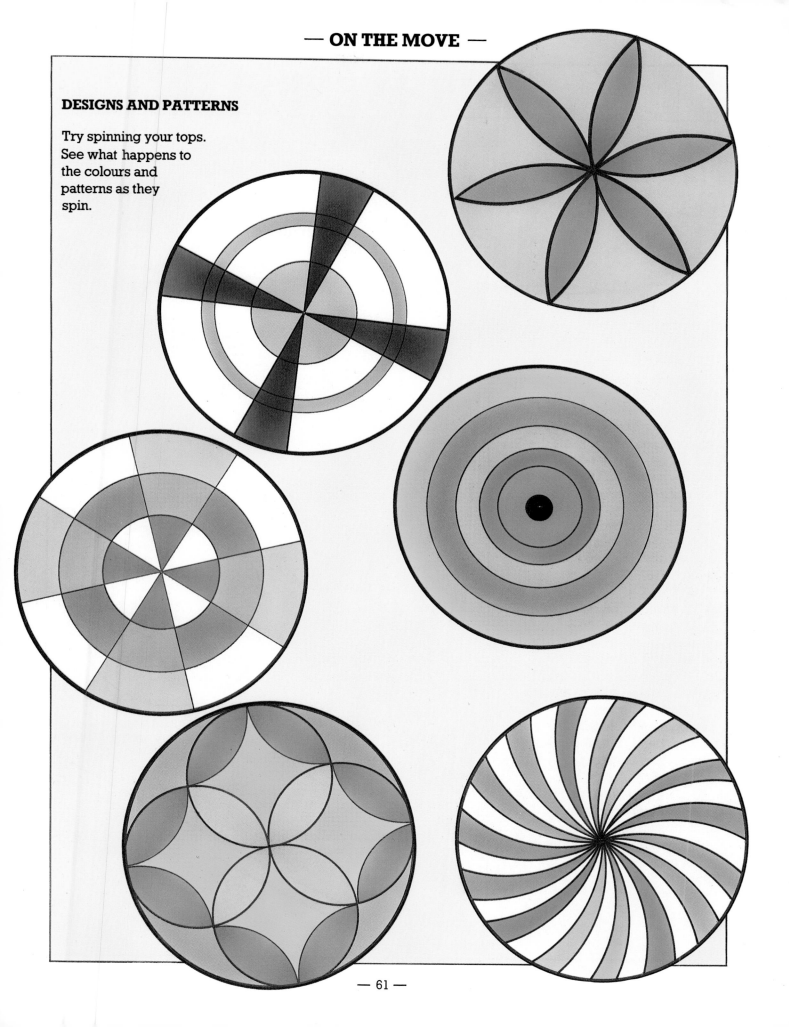

DESIGNS AND PATTERNS

Try spinning your tops.
See what happens to
the colours and
patterns as they
spin.

SPINNERS

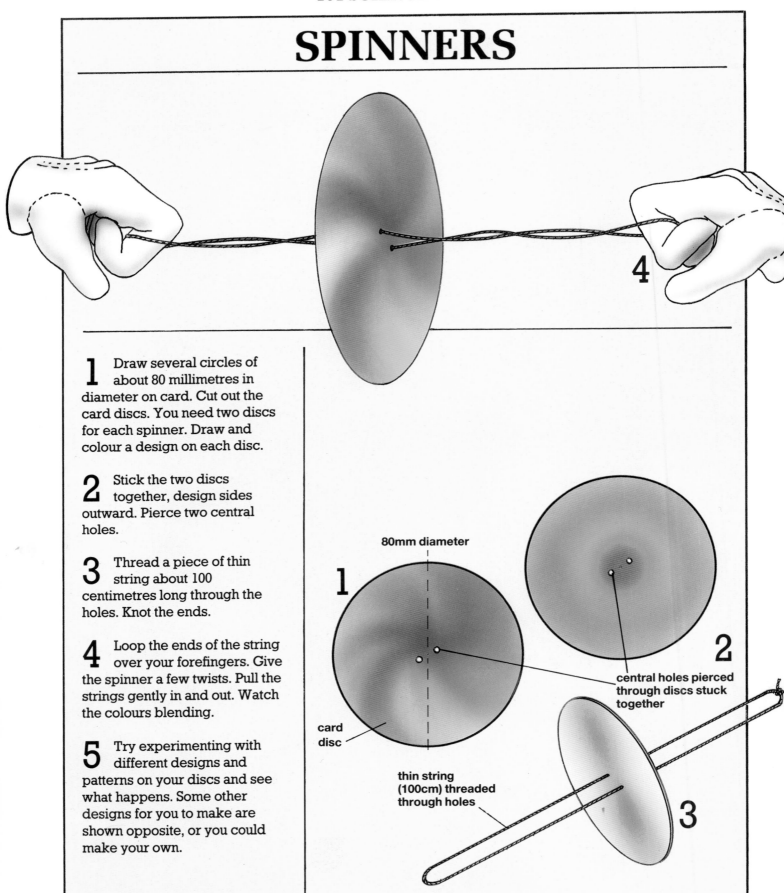

1 Draw several circles of about 80 millimetres in diameter on card. Cut out the card discs. You need two discs for each spinner. Draw and colour a design on each disc.

2 Stick the two discs together, design sides outward. Pierce two central holes.

3 Thread a piece of thin string about 100 centimetres long through the holes. Knot the ends.

4 Loop the ends of the string over your forefingers. Give the spinner a few twists. Pull the strings gently in and out. Watch the colours blending.

5 Try experimenting with different designs and patterns on your discs and see what happens. Some other designs for you to make are shown opposite, or you could make your own.

80mm diameter

1 card disc

2 central holes pierced through discs stuck together

3 thin string (100cm) threaded through holes

MAKE OTHER DESIGNS

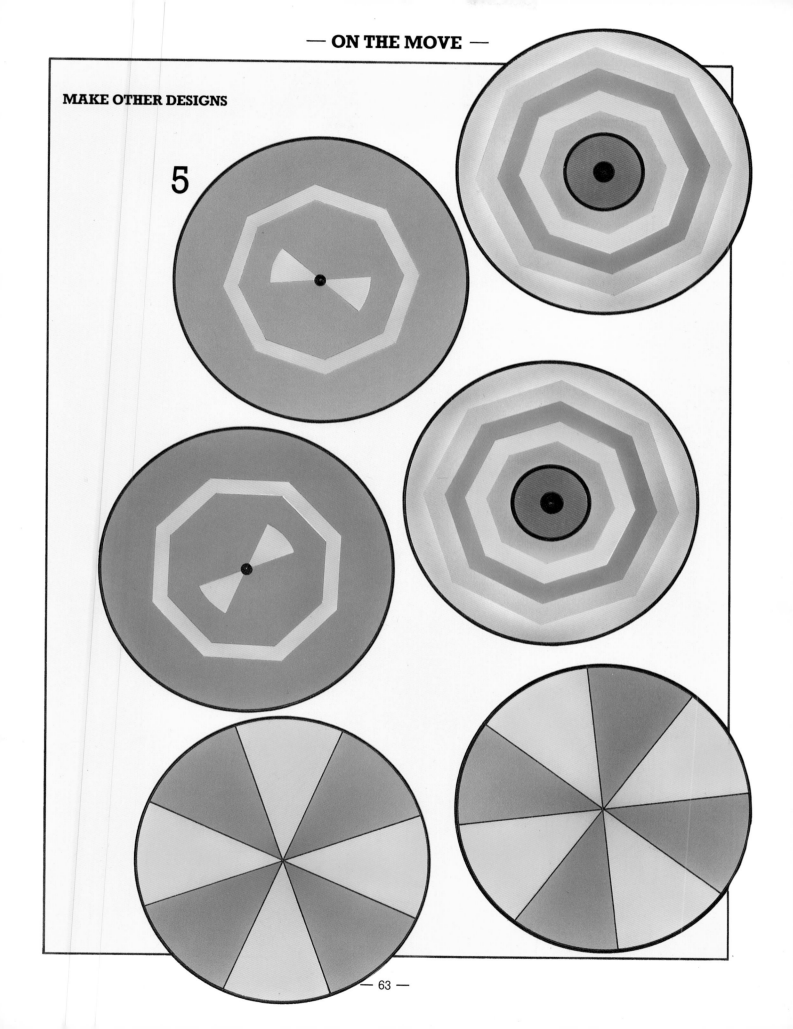

PAPER BOAT

1 Use a sheet of greaseproof paper 200 millimetres square. Fold the sides to the middle.

2 Fold in the corners to the middle.

3 Make creases, as shown, and fold in.

4 Crease horizontally across, as shown, and fold in.

5 Turn the boat over – inside out so to speak!

Float the boat along a stream or in the bath.

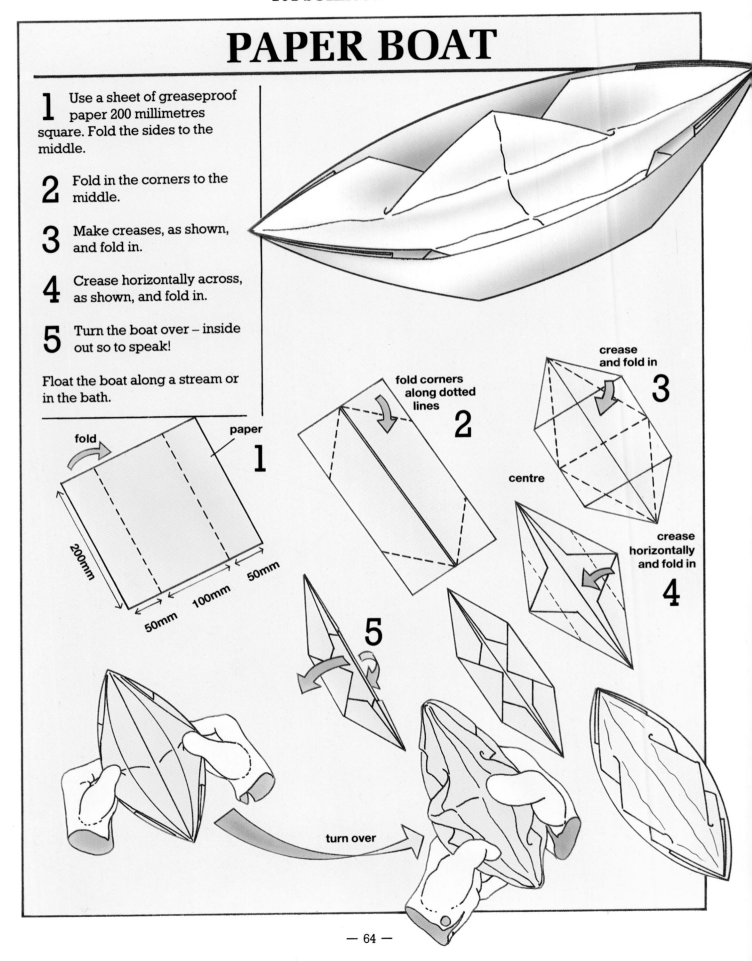

BALSA WOOD BOATS

1 You need some balsa wood to make the bases or 'hulls' of your boats. Look at the different shaped hulls below and choose some shapes to try. Cut them out.

2 Make sails for your boats with knitting needles and paper. Look at the different shaped sails below and choose some shapes to try. Cut out the sails from paper and attach them to your hulls with knitting needles.

Small sails for small boats can be made from cocktail sticks and paper.

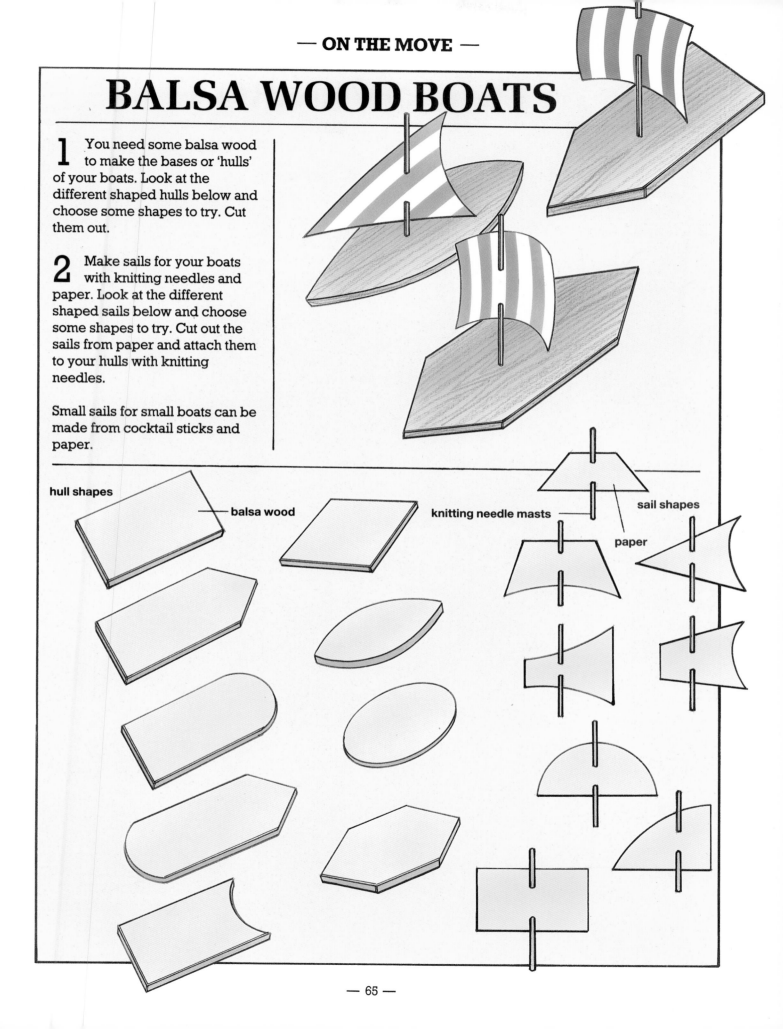

hull shapes

balsa wood

knitting needle masts

sail shapes

paper

POWER-DRIVEN BOATS

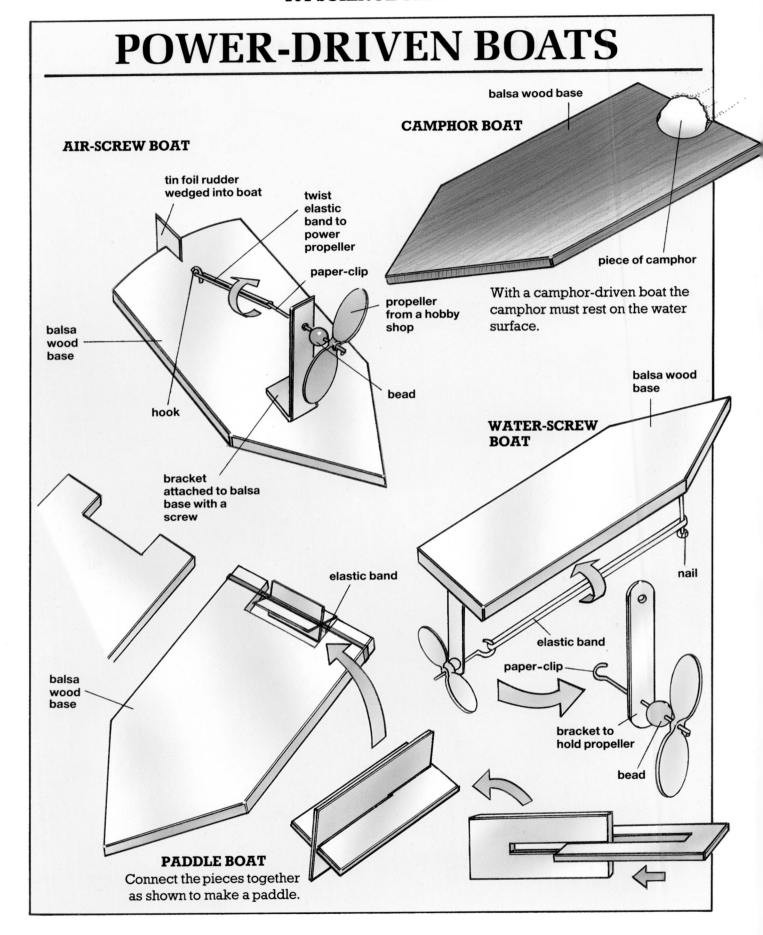

CAMPHOR BOAT

balsa wood base

piece of camphor

With a camphor-driven boat the camphor must rest on the water surface.

AIR-SCREW BOAT

tin foil rudder wedged into boat

twist elastic band to power propeller

paper-clip

propeller from a hobby shop

bead

balsa wood base

hook

bracket attached to balsa base with a screw

WATER-SCREW BOAT

balsa wood base

nail

elastic band

elastic band

paper-clip

bracket to hold propeller

bead

balsa wood base

PADDLE BOAT
Connect the pieces together as shown to make a paddle.

CATAMARAN AND TRIMARAN

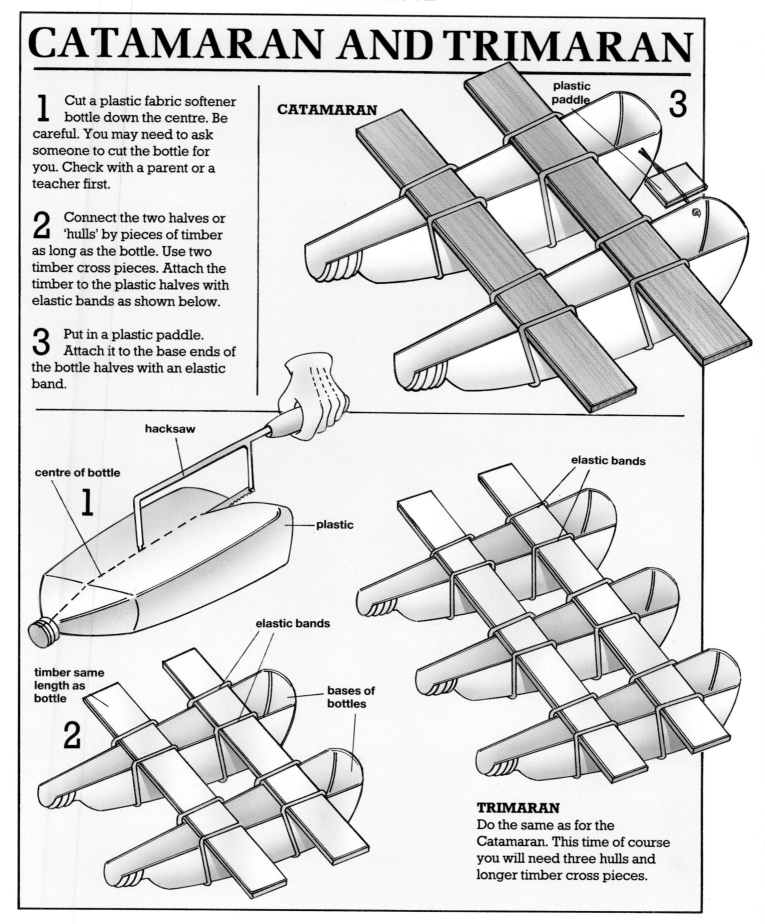

1 Cut a plastic fabric softener bottle down the centre. Be careful. You may need to ask someone to cut the bottle for you. Check with a parent or a teacher first.

2 Connect the two halves or 'hulls' by pieces of timber as long as the bottle. Use two timber cross pieces. Attach the timber to the plastic halves with elastic bands as shown below.

3 Put in a plastic paddle. Attach it to the base ends of the bottle halves with an elastic band.

CATAMARAN

plastic paddle

3

hacksaw

centre of bottle

1

plastic

timber same length as bottle

2

elastic bands

bases of bottles

elastic bands

TRIMARAN
Do the same as for the Catamaran. This time of course you will need three hulls and longer timber cross pieces.

NOTES FOR PARENTS AND TEACHERS

Pages 39 – 53   These are concerned with things in the air. If you want to consider the forces that keep paper planes in the air you will need to talk with children about thrust, drag, lift and gravity. Thrust is provided by the aeroplane engine. In a paper plane, of course, it is provided by throwing. Drag is the resistance of the air to flight. It acts along the direction of motion of the aeroplane and opposes it. Lift is another force, it acts more or less perpendicularly to the direction of motion. The shape of an aeroplane wing helps develop lift. Gravity is the pull of the earth acting on the plane.

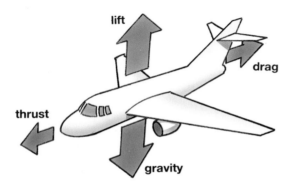

Page 45   Both the models on this page use a form of energy to make them move. The air escaping from the balloon causes it to move forward. To every action there is an equal and opposite reaction. When the balloon is blown up but shut the air inside it presses equally in all directions. When the neck is released the air rushes out and there is no longer any backward pressure. The forward pressure of air on the balloon remains the same however and it travels forward.

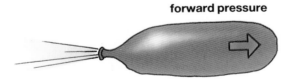

The propeller-driven plane moves on 'elastic energy'. Children will have to put the 'energy' in first by winding it up.

Pages 46 – 47   Air pressure is the operative force in making these two models work.

Page 48   The aerodynamics of boomerangs are extremely complex, which is not to say that children cannot get a 'feel' for what is happening by playing with these models.

Page 49   Again we have a toy which works on air pressure.

Pages 50 – 51   The spinning blades from these helicopters cut the air and their curved shape gives them lift, much as an aeroplane wing does.

Do please supervise these activities.

Page 52   The kite, like the aeroplane, is subjected to forces. The energy to lift it provided by the wind, whilst its angle to the wind gives it lift. Like aeroplanes it is subjected to the pull of gravity.

Page 53   Hot-air balloons work on the principle that warm air is less dense than cold air (the molecules are further apart). Being filled with warm air the balloons therefore tend to lift displacing the colder, denser air above them.

Pages 54 – 55   Two toys which are very much concerned with 'elastic energy'. If children are interested you can experiment with the number of turns of the elastic in relation to the distance travelled by each vehicle.

Page 56   Angle of attack of the wind is all important in getting a high speed from the land yacht – and it can travel! So encourage children to get the best angle with their boom.

Page 57   Introduces children to the idea of using an electric motor to make things move.

Pages 58 – 59   Both the jumping Jack and the mouse are based on the principle of the lever. That is to say they are both dependent on the effect of a bar moving about a point.

Pages 60 – 63   You have to put energy into tops to make them spin. Colours in the surface of the top will blend. Theoretically if you have a rainbow coloured top all the colours should merge to give white. In practice, this is impossible since one cannot get pure enough pigments. At best you will get a grey blur. The same applies to the spinners.

Pages 64 – 67   Lots of variables here for children to play with in order to get the best boat. Shapes of hull and sail, and power source whether it be blowing or propeller driven by elastic all come into effect.

Camphor reduces the surface tension of the water and the 'water skin' in front of the boat pulls it forward.

3
on
Paper

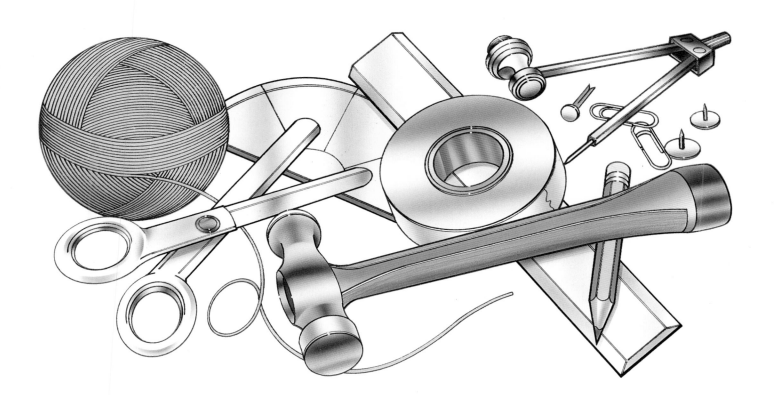

INTRODUCTION

In **On Paper** you will find out about some of the amazing things that you can make and do with paper and card. Have you ever heard of paper making a noise? Try frightening your friends with a bull roarer! Did you know that a simple fold in a piece of paper can help you to tell the time? Try making your very own pocket sundial. Did you know that heat can make things move? Find out how to use heat to create a revolving fairy for the top of the Christmas tree. Choosing a card to send to one of your friends is always a problem, but what about making some of your own, and making action ones at that! Long ago the Ancient Chinese discovered lots of exciting ways of making interesting patterns with numbers and shapes. They even discovered some which they thought were magical. Try making them for yourself and see what you think. These are just a few of the exciting things that you can make or do with paper. Everything that you need is listed on page 101.

PLAYING CARDS

Try building things with cards.

1 Build a house of cards. Lean two cards together to make a tent shape. Make another tent shape alongside and then put a card across the top. Continue in this way to build the bottom layer. Build a second layer on top of the first. Can you use all the cards in the pack without it toppling over?

2 How tall a tower can you build with six cards as your base? How tall a tower can you build on just three cards as a base?

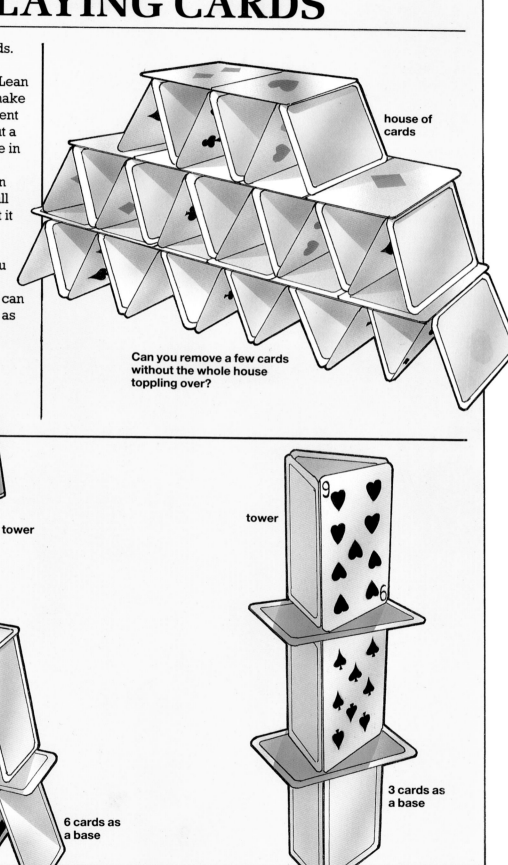

house of cards

Can you remove a few cards without the whole house toppling over?

tower

6 cards as a base

tower

3 cards as a base

BALANCING BILL

1 Trace the figure of Balancing Bill onto thick card. Cut it out.

2 You will now need to balance him. Use a tightrope made from thin string tied between two plastic bottles filled with sand or soil. Attach Bill to the tightrope. He may balance, he may fall off. If he falls off you need to make some counterbalances.

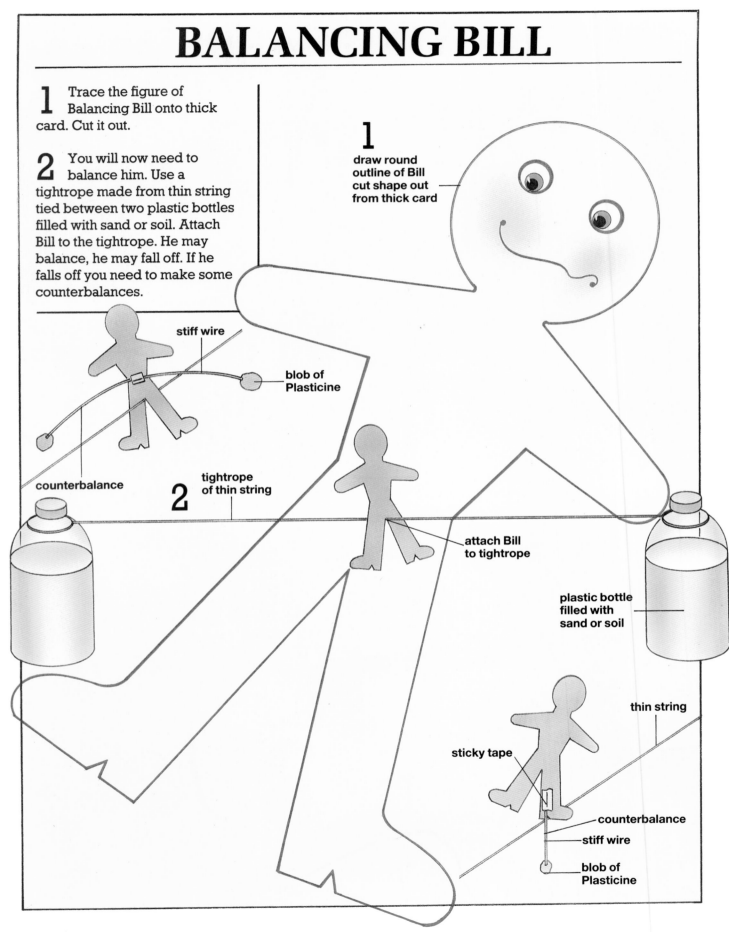

1 draw round outline of Bill cut shape out from thick card

stiff wire

blob of Plasticine

counterbalance

2 tightrope of thin string

attach Bill to tightrope

plastic bottle filled with sand or soil

sticky tape

thin string

counterbalance

stiff wire

blob of Plasticine

BALANCING JILL

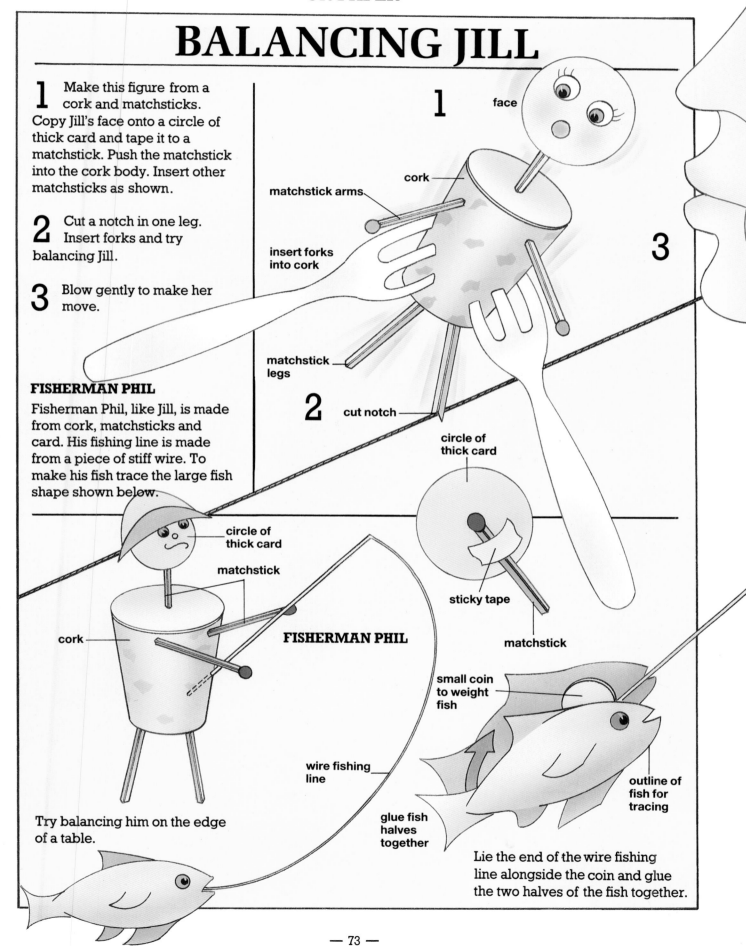

1 Make this figure from a cork and matchsticks. Copy Jill's face onto a circle of thick card and tape it to a matchstick. Push the matchstick into the cork body. Insert other matchsticks as shown.

2 Cut a notch in one leg. Insert forks and try balancing Jill.

3 Blow gently to make her move.

face

cork

matchstick arms

insert forks into cork

matchstick legs

cut notch

circle of thick card

sticky tape

matchstick

1

2

3

FISHERMAN PHIL

Fisherman Phil, like Jill, is made from cork, matchsticks and card. His fishing line is made from a piece of stiff wire. To make his fish trace the large fish shape shown below.

circle of thick card

matchstick

cork

FISHERMAN PHIL

Try balancing him on the edge of a table.

small coin to weight fish

wire fishing line

glue fish halves together

outline of fish for tracing

Lie the end of the wire fishing line alongside the coin and glue the two halves of the fish together.

FEARSOME FRED

1 Trace and cut the large face of Fred from thick card and colour it in.

2 Balance him on the end of a ruler or the edge of a table as shown below. Use a paper-clip to help you get a good balance. You need to move it about to find the best balancing point.

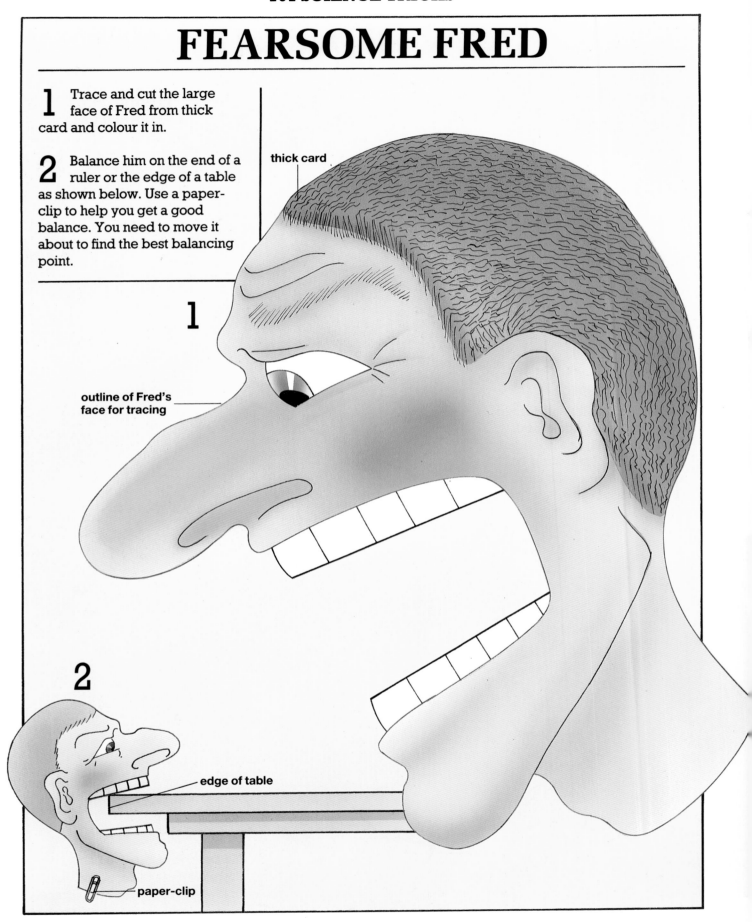

thick card

1

outline of Fred's face for tracing

2

edge of table

paper-clip

BALANCING BOYS

This toy is made from card, balsa wood, wire and Plasticine.

1 Shape a piece of balsa wood, as shown.

2 Draw and cut the see-saw and the two boys from card. Colour them in. Glue the boys to the see-saw and the see-saw to the balsa wood pivot.

3 Shape a piece of Plasticine into a ball. Attach it to the stiff wire to make a counterweight as shown. This will help you get a good balance.

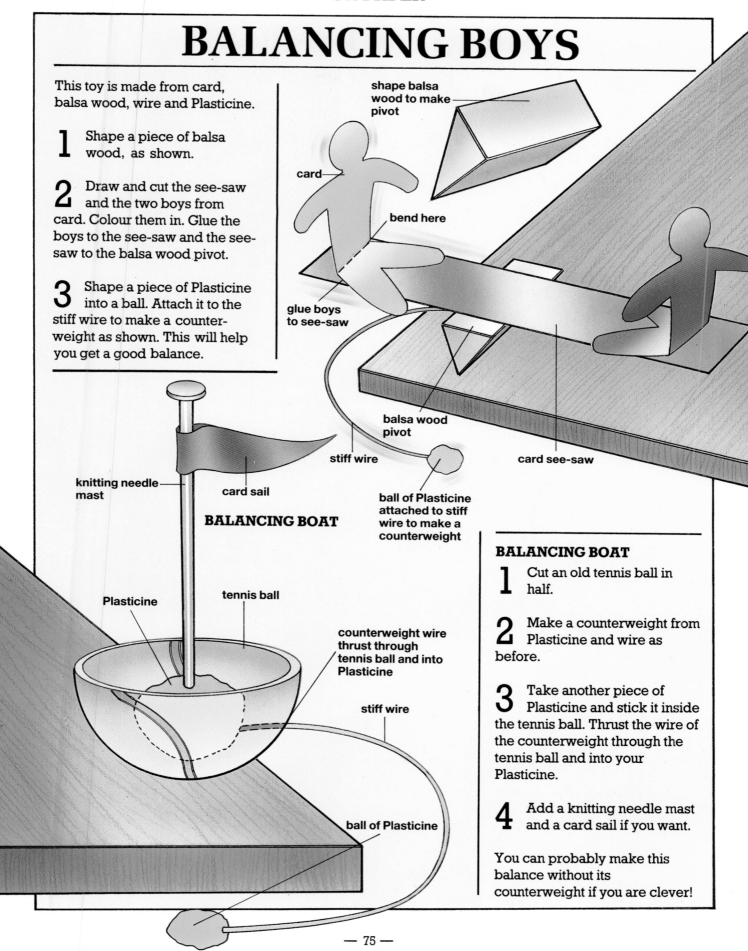

shape balsa wood to make pivot

card

bend here

glue boys to see-saw

balsa wood pivot

stiff wire

card see-saw

ball of Plasticine attached to stiff wire to make a counterweight

knitting needle mast

card sail

BALANCING BOAT

Plasticine

tennis ball

counterweight wire thrust through tennis ball and into Plasticine

stiff wire

ball of Plasticine

BALANCING BOAT

1 Cut an old tennis ball in half.

2 Make a counterweight from Plasticine and wire as before.

3 Take another piece of Plasticine and stick it inside the tennis ball. Thrust the wire of the counterweight through the tennis ball and into your Plasticine.

4 Add a knitting needle mast and a card sail if you want.

You can probably make this balance without its counterweight if you are clever!

BULL ROARER

1 Cut a piece of heavy cardboard about 200 millimetres long by 50 millimetres wide. Round off the corners. Punch a hole at one end and thread a metre of string through. Tie securely.

2 Twist the bull roarer so that you give it a slight bend.

3 Find a clear space. Swing it around your head. It will roar like a bull.

Decorate your bull roarer if you want.

You could have a competition with your friends to see who can make the loudest bull roarer.

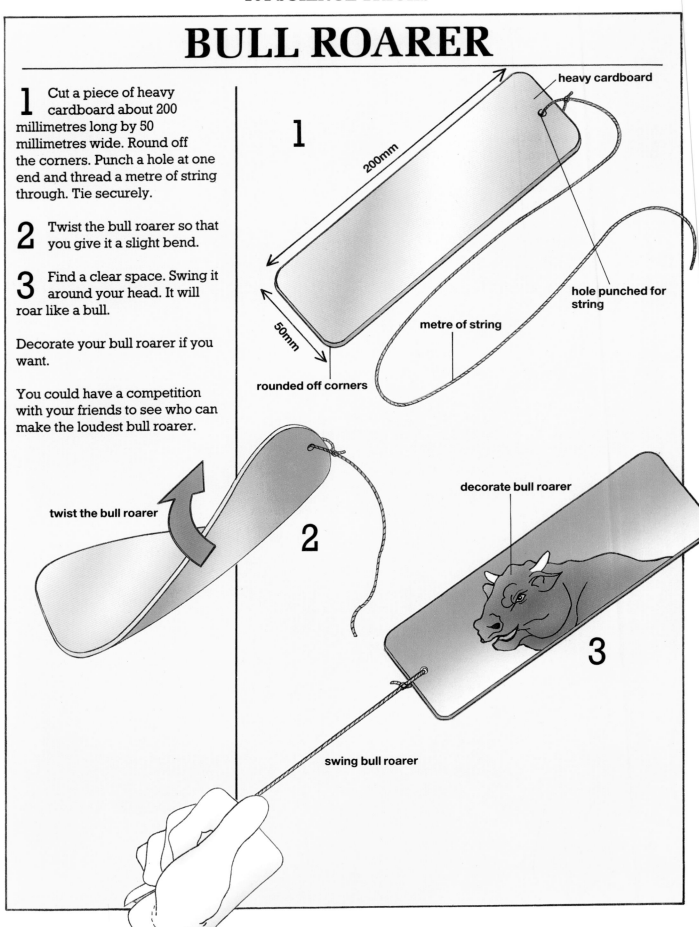

1

heavy cardboard

200mm

hole punched for string

50mm

metre of string

rounded off corners

twist the bull roarer

2

decorate bull roarer

3

swing bull roarer

BUZZ SAW

1 Trace the pattern below onto stiff card. Colour it in and cut it out.

2 Punch two holes through the card. Use the point of a a pair of compasses.

3 Thread a metre of thin string through the holes. Tie the ends.

4 Loop the ends of the string over your fingers. Pull the string outwards and then relax. Keep repeating this. The buzz saw will spin. Hold the revolving buzz saw to a sheet of paper sticking out from a table. As the teeth of the buzz saw hit the paper you will hear a buzzing noise.

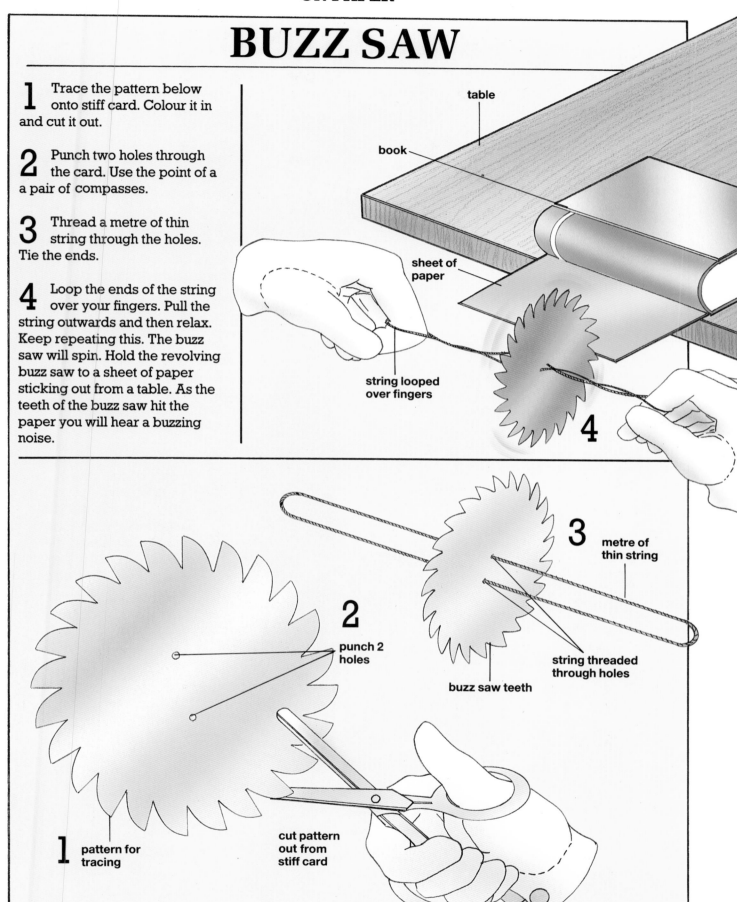

table

book

sheet of paper

string looped over fingers

4

2

punch 2 holes

3

metre of thin string

string threaded through holes

buzz saw teeth

1 pattern for tracing

cut pattern out from stiff card

POCKET SUNDIAL

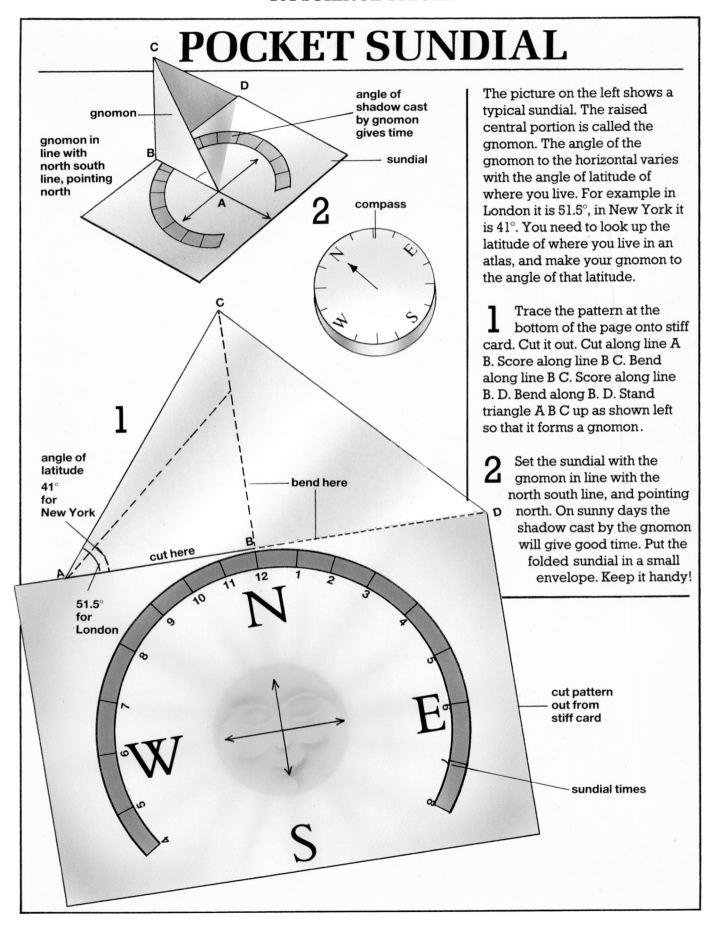

gnomon

gnomon in line with north south line, pointing north

C

D

angle of shadow cast by gnomon gives time

sundial

B

A

2

compass

N

E

W

S

The picture on the left shows a typical sundial. The raised central portion is called the gnomon. The angle of the gnomon to the horizontal varies with the angle of latitude of where you live. For example in London it is 51.5°, in New York it is 41°. You need to look up the latitude of where you live in an atlas, and make your gnomon to the angle of that latitude.

1 Trace the pattern at the bottom of the page onto stiff card. Cut it out. Cut along line A B. Score along line B C. Bend along line B C. Score along line B. D. Bend along B. D. Stand triangle A B C up as shown left so that it forms a gnomon.

2 Set the sundial with the gnomon in line with the north south line, and pointing north. On sunny days the shadow cast by the gnomon will give good time. Put the folded sundial in a small envelope. Keep it handy!

C

1

angle of latitude 41° for New York

bend here

cut here

B

A

51.5° for London

D

cut pattern out from stiff card

10 11 12 1 2 3 4 5 6

9 8 7

N

E

W

S

sundial times

STAR CLOCK

1 Cut a 150 millimetre disc from card and draw a 100 millimetre circle on it. Mark out 30 degree sectors with a protractor on the 100 millimetre circle. Draw in the Plough, Cassiopeia and the Pole Star as shown.

2 Cut a 200 millimetre disc from card and draw a 150 millimetre circle on it. Mark out a 24 hour clock on this large disc.

3 Fix the small disc to the large disc with a paper fastener. At night match the star circle with the Plough constellation in the sky. Note the time and arrange the clock circle against the pointers of the Plough.

An hour later check the position of the Plough. Match the star circle to the Plough again. You will find it rotates to your 24 hour clock.

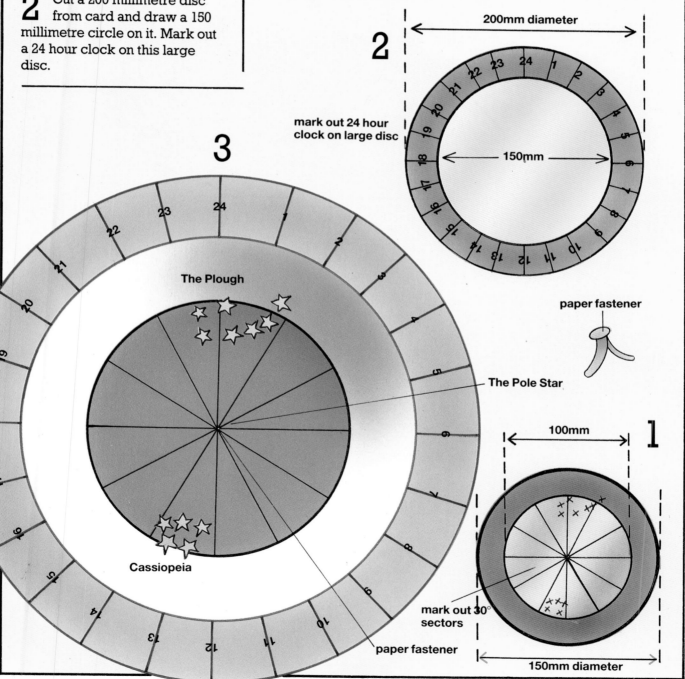

2 200mm diameter

mark out 24 hour clock on large disc

150mm

3

The Plough

The Pole Star

paper fastener

Cassiopeia

1 100mm

mark out 30° sectors

paper fastener

150mm diameter

REVOLVING SNAKE

1 Trace this snake onto thin card or paper.

2 Cut it out. Cut along the line of the snake.

3 Make a pin prick through the snake's tail.

Thread cotton through the hole. Tie two or three knots.

4 Hold the snake above the table lamp. The heat current rising from the lamp will cause the snake to revolve.

A snake hung above a radiator will turn all day – if the radiator is left on.

1

outline of snake

thin card or paper

cut along outline of snake

2

thread cotton through hole in snake's tail

3

4

heat current causes snake to revolve

lamp

CHRISTMAS TREE FAIRY

Cut a snake as before but this time use aluminium kitchen foil.

1 Trace the shape shown below to make the fairy. Cut this from kitchen foil too but make it double thickness for strength.

2 Leave an extended piece that can be bent back to make a base.

3 Use a popper as a bearing. Stick the popper to the base of the fairy with a touch of adhesive.

4 Stick the foil snake to the popper by its head. Use a

needle pushed into the end of a balsa wood rod as a pivot for the fairy.

The fairy will revolve well on the Christmas Tree if a clutch of fairy lights are put just beneath it.

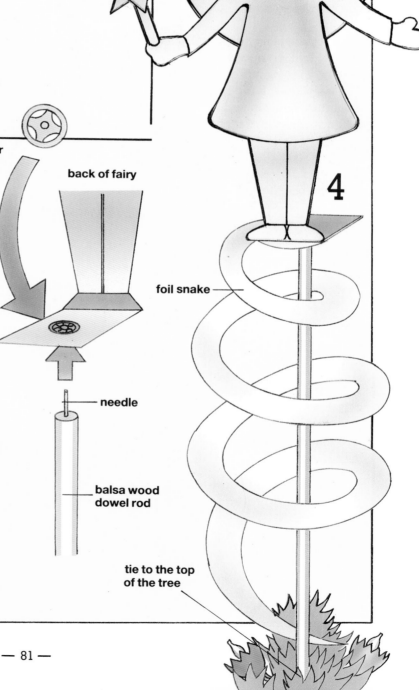

1

2 layers of aluminium foil

outline of fairy

3 stick popper to base of fairy

back of fairy

4

foil snake

needle

balsa wood dowel rod

2

extended piece

base

bend back to make base

tie to the top of the tree

MAGIC SQUARES

Magic squares were invented many centuries ago by the Chinese. The earliest form is shown on the right, the 'lo-shu' as it is called. Can you see what is magic about it? Count the dots in each row, column and both diagonals.

1 Whether you add up, down or across the answer always comes to 15. Three times the central number.

This square is so magical that people still wear it as a lucky charm. This is an order 3 magic square since it has 3 rows and 3 columns. You can make lots of order 3 squares to try on your friends.

2 Add 3 to every number in the original square.

The answers to the additions are 24. That is to say three times the central number.

Try adding other numbers.

3 Multiply every number in the original square by 4.

The answer to the additions is 60. Three times the central number.

Try multiplying by other numbers.

the earliest form of magic square is called the 'lo-shu'

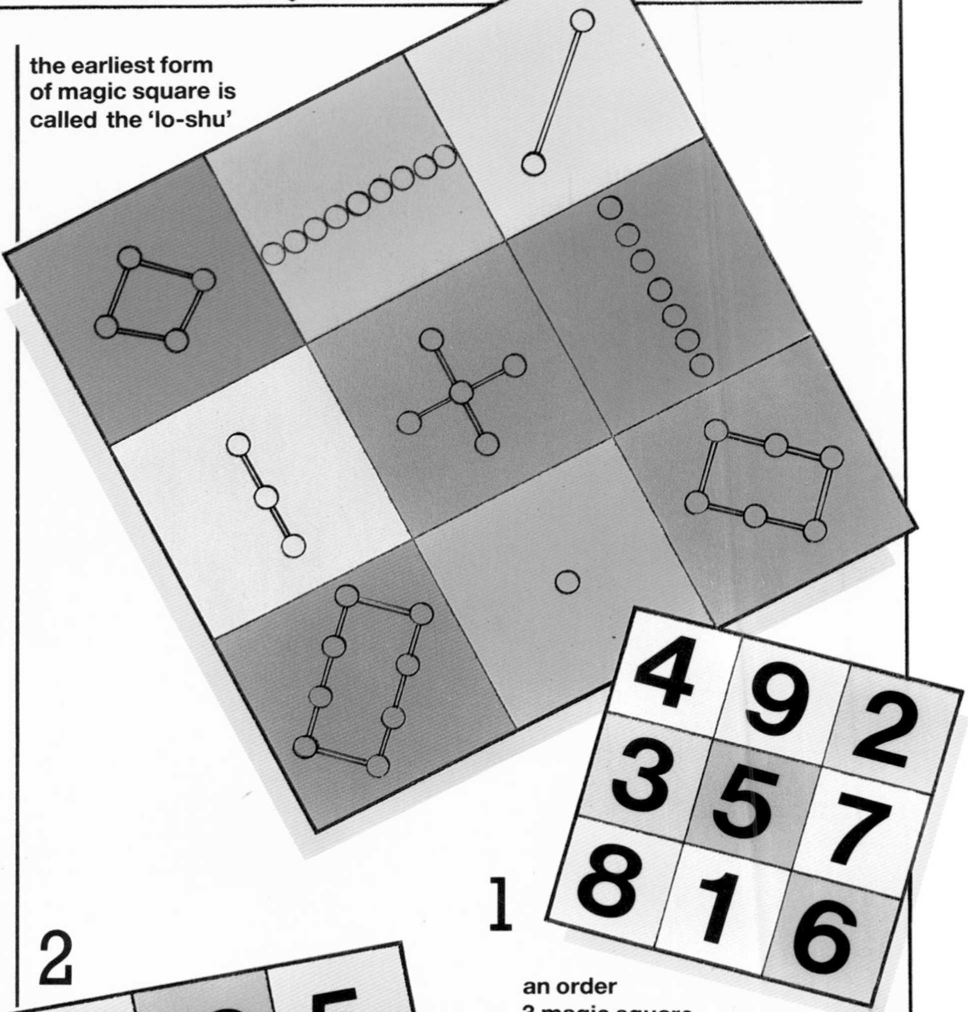

4	9	2
3	5	7
8	1	6

1 an order 3 magic square

2

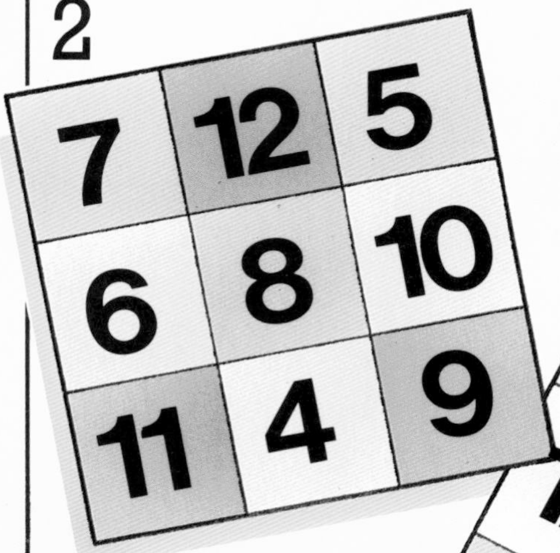

7	12	5
6	8	10
11	4	9

Add 3 to every number in the original square.

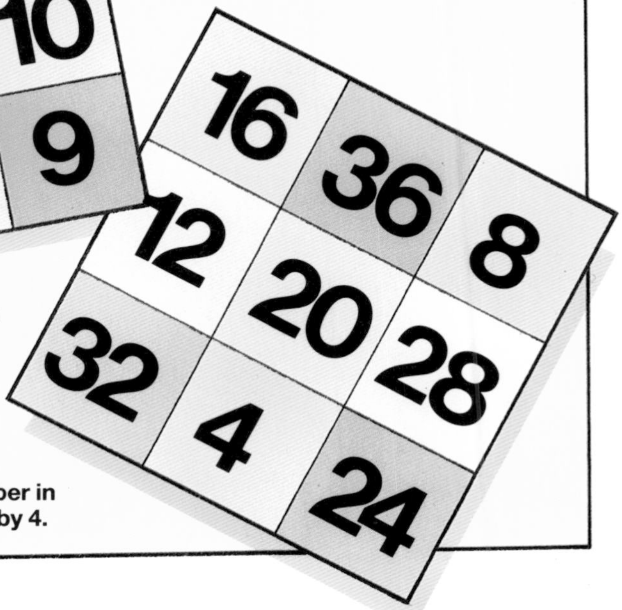

16	36	8
12	20	28
32	4	24

3 Multiply every number in the original square by 4.

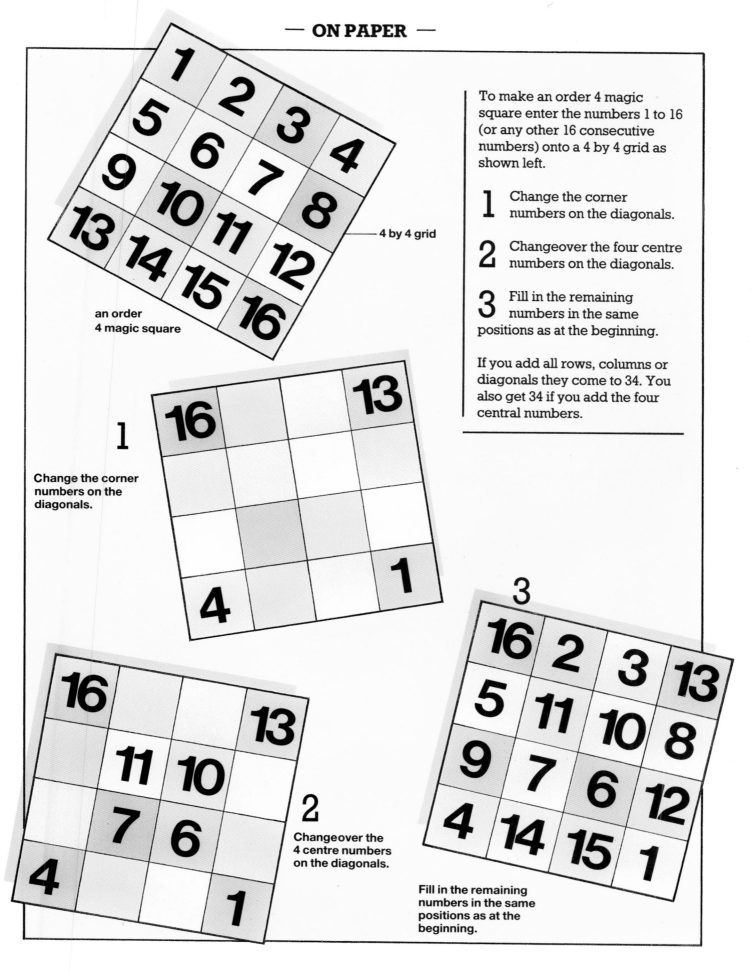

an order
4 magic square

4 by 4 grid

To make an order 4 magic square enter the numbers 1 to 16 (or any other 16 consecutive numbers) onto a 4 by 4 grid as shown left.

1   Change the corner numbers on the diagonals.

2   Changeover the four centre numbers on the diagonals.

3   Fill in the remaining numbers in the same positions as at the beginning.

If you add all rows, columns or diagonals they come to 34. You also get 34 if you add the four central numbers.

1

Change the corner numbers on the diagonals.

2

Changeover the 4 centre numbers on the diagonals.

3

Fill in the remaining numbers in the same positions as at the beginning.

TANGRAMS

Another Chinese invention is the tangram. It is a seven piece puzzle.

1 It is easily constructed if you use the sixteen square grid shown to help you draw the seven pieces. These then need to be cut out. You could colour them in if you like.

2 Can you remake the square from the seven pieces?

3 The Chinese use the pieces to make all sorts of figures like the examples below. You try.

square

16 square grid

cut out the 7 pieces from card

more tangrams to make

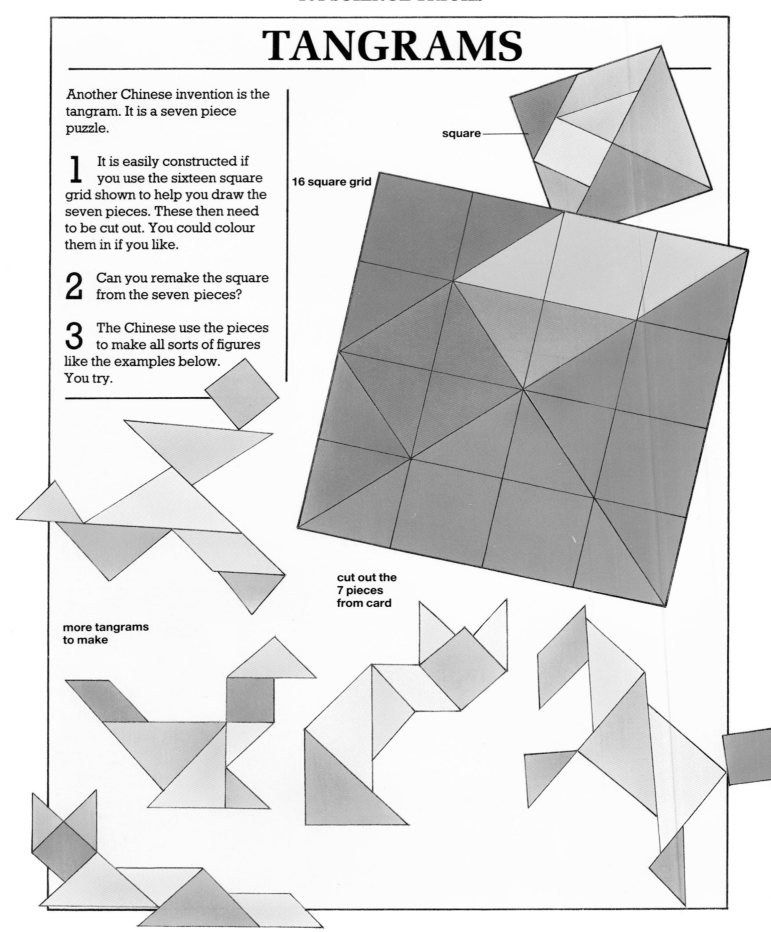

MAGIC EGGS

1 Trace the template of the magic egg onto card.

2 Cut out the seven pieces and colour them in.

3 What birds can you hatch using your seven pieces?

template of egg for tracing

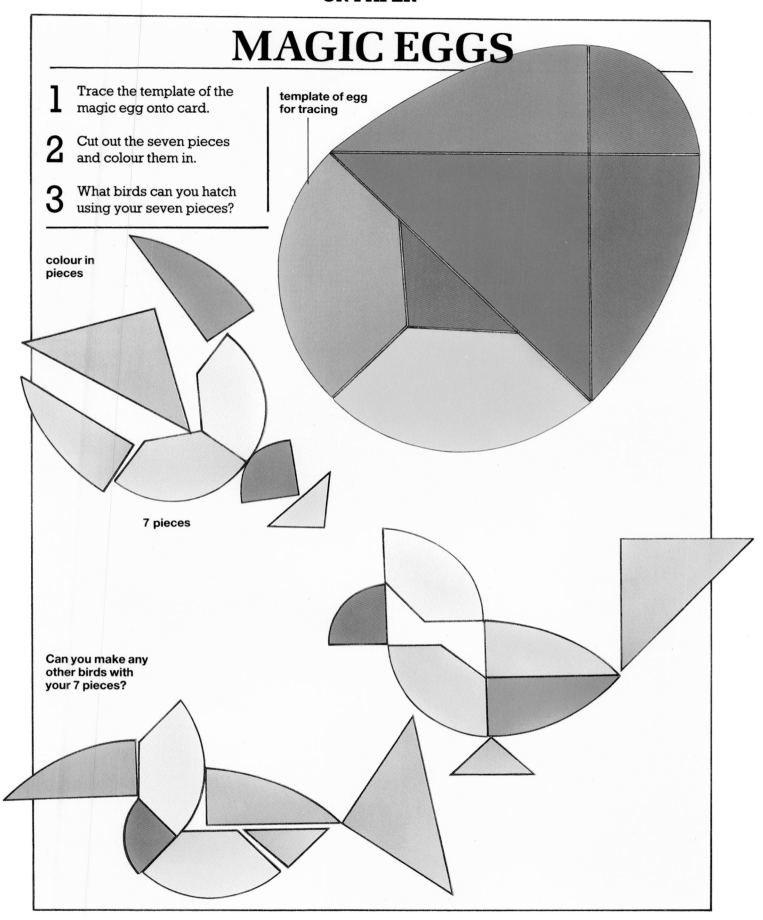

colour in pieces

7 pieces

Can you make any other birds with your 7 pieces?

3-D DESK CALENDAR

1 Trace this 5 sided shape called a pentagon onto card. Cut it out to make a template.

2 Draw round the template to construct the two nets shown below on thick paper or thin card. Remember to draw the flaps too.

3 Cut out the nets. Fold all the flaps and score along all the sides of the inner pentagon.

4 Glue the two nets together to make a 12 sided shape called a dodecahedron.

5 Each face of the dodecahedron will hold the calendar for one month of the year. Write one month on each face. You may find it easier to write up your calendar before you join your two nets together.

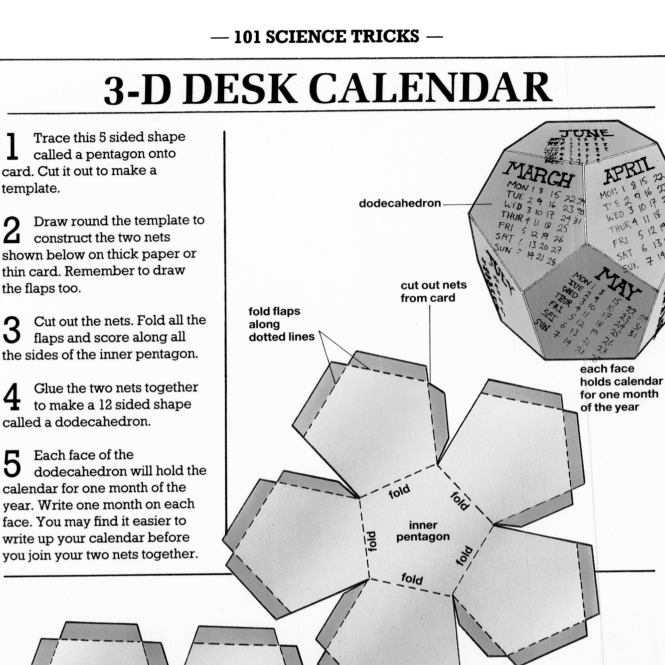

dodecahedron

cut out nets from card

fold flaps along dotted lines

fold
fold
fold
inner pentagon
fold
fold

each face holds calendar for one month of the year

fold **fold**
fold **fold**
fold

template of pentagon

JANUARY
MON	1	8	15	22	29
TUE	2	9	16	23	30
WED	3	10	17	24	31
THUR	4	11	18	25	
FRI	5	12	19	26	
SAT	6	13	20	27	
SUN	7	14	21	28	

OTHER 3-D SHAPES

The dodecahedron is a regular solid. There are four other regular solids: the cube, tetrahedron, octahedron and icosahedron. The nets for each of these solids are shown below.

1 Trace each net onto thin card. Cut it out. Score along all the dotted lines.

2 Shape and glue each solid. When they are made you can hang them by cotton from a shelf. You can hang a dodecahedron too.

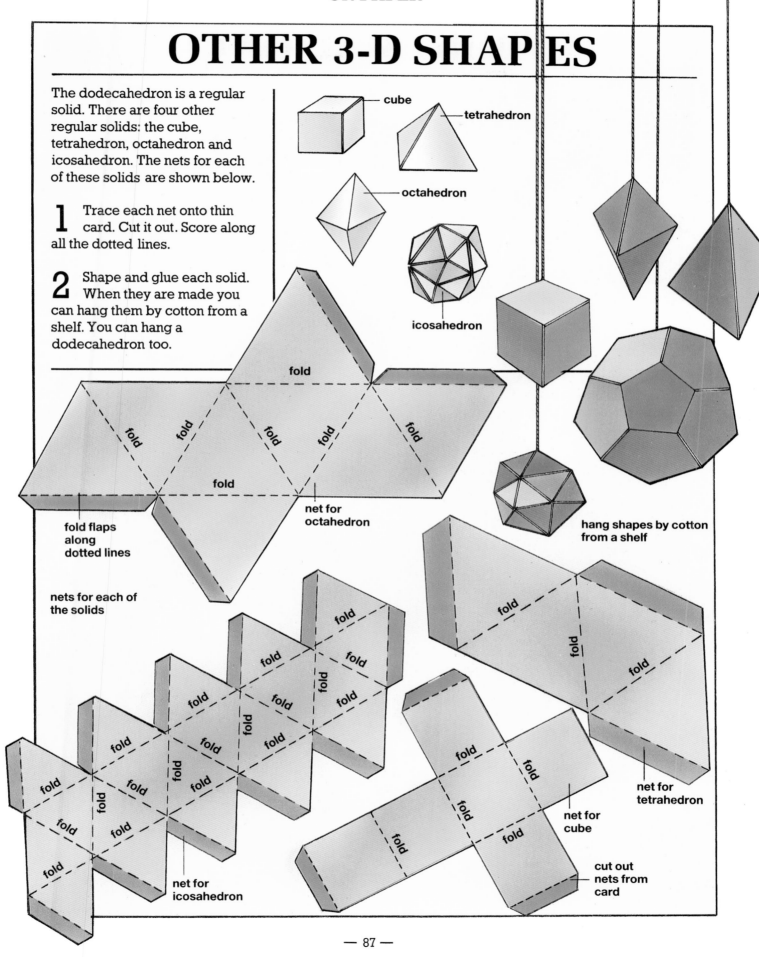

cube

tetrahedron

octahedron

icosahedron

hang shapes by cotton from a shelf

fold
fold
fold
fold
fold
fold
fold

net for octahedron

fold flaps along dotted lines

nets for each of the solids

fold
fold
fold
fold
fold
fold
fold
fold
fold
fold
fold
fold
fold
fold
fold
fold
fold
fold

net for icosahedron

fold
fold
fold
fold
fold

net for cube

fold
fold
fold

net for tetrahedron

cut out nets from card

CHRISTMAS CARD

1 Trace and cut out these four templates A, B, C, D from card.

2 Cut out the two slits in template D as shown.

3 Colour in Santa Claus, template A.

4 Thread the long narrow strip C through the two slits in the large card D. Stick Santa Claus to strip C. Lightly glue the fireplace B to each side of the card. Let it dry.

5 Pull on the strip to make Santa Claus appear. Push on the strip to send him back up the chimney. Decorate the chimney breast.

templates for tracing

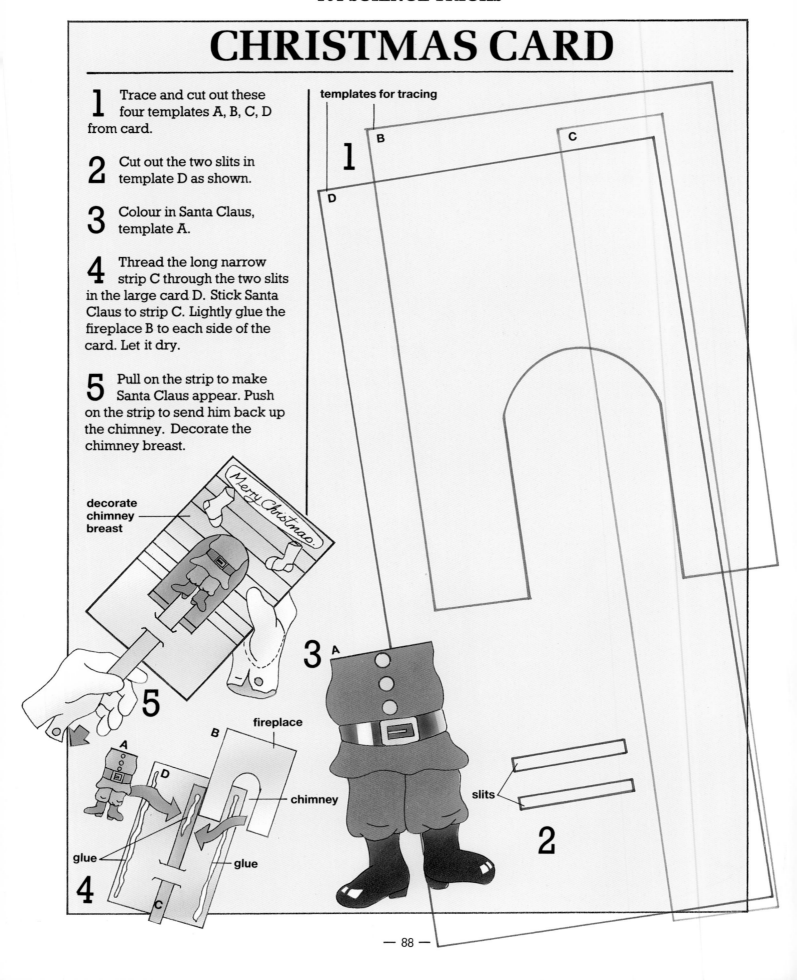

decorate chimney breast

Merry Christmas.

fireplace

chimney

glue

glue

slits

GET WELL CARD

1 Trace and cut these templates A B C below from card. Cut out the shaded portions on the large card A.

2 Draw the mouse on the narrow strip of card C.

3 Fix the small card oblong B at the back of the large card A with a touch of glue at the top and at the bottom.

Assemble.

4 Push and pull the strip to make the mouse appear and disappear.

Decorate the card.

templates for tracing

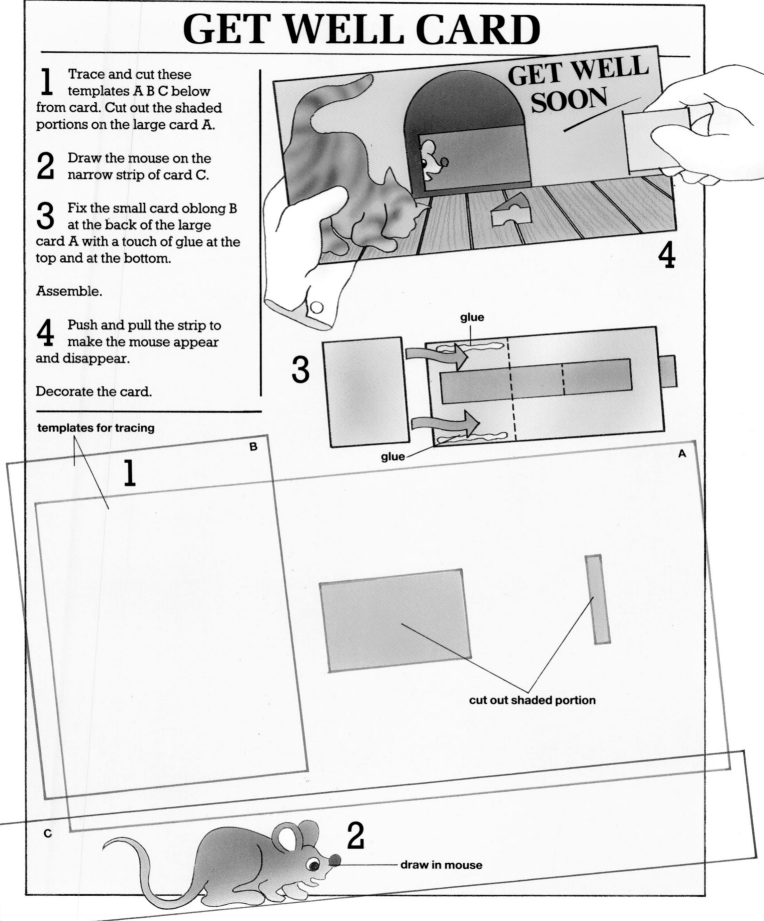

GET WELL SOON

4

3 glue

glue

1 B

A

cut out shaded portion

C

2

draw in mouse

NEW YEAR CARD

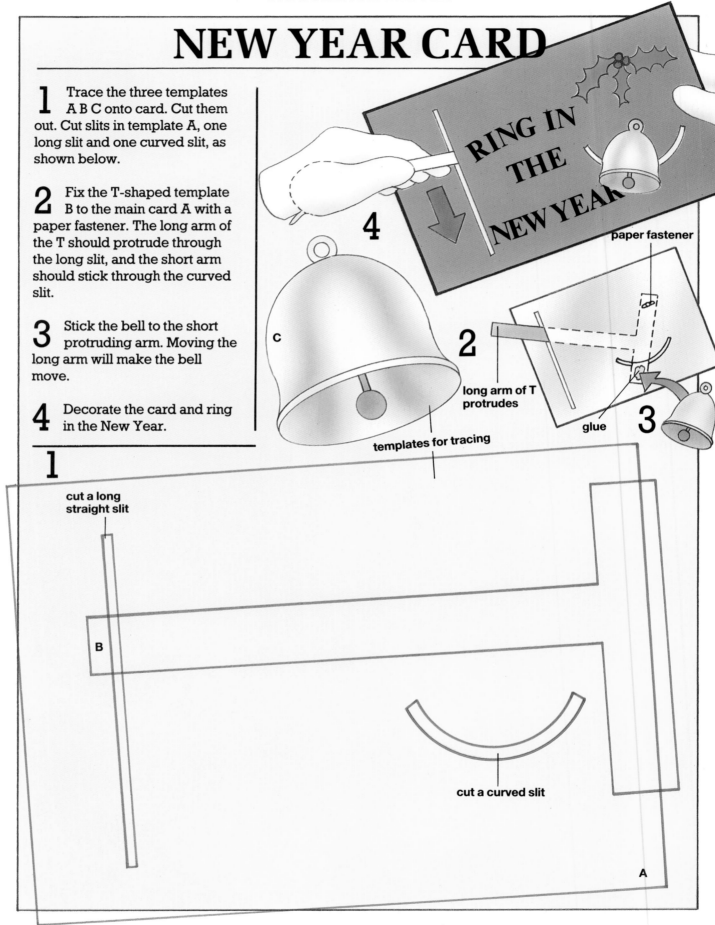

1 Trace the three templates A B C onto card. Cut them out. Cut slits in template A, one long slit and one curved slit, as shown below.

2 Fix the T-shaped template B to the main card A with a paper fastener. The long arm of the T should protrude through the long slit, and the short arm should stick through the curved slit.

3 Stick the bell to the short protruding arm. Moving the long arm will make the bell move.

4 Decorate the card and ring in the New Year.

RING IN THE NEW YEAR

paper fastener

long arm of T protrudes

glue

templates for tracing

C

cut a long straight slit

B

cut a curved slit

A

MOBILES

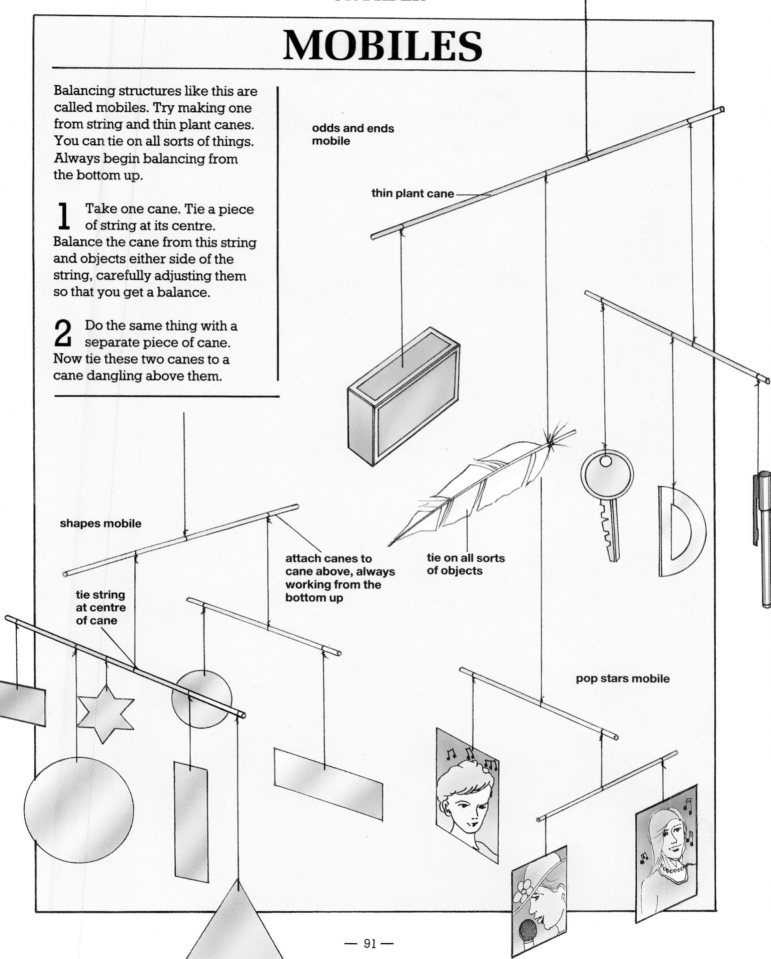

Balancing structures like this are called mobiles. Try making one from string and thin plant canes. You can tie on all sorts of things. Always begin balancing from the bottom up.

1 Take one cane. Tie a piece of string at its centre. Balance the cane from this string and objects either side of the string, carefully adjusting them so that you get a balance.

2 Do the same thing with a separate piece of cane. Now tie these two canes to a cane dangling above them.

odds and ends mobile

thin plant cane

shapes mobile

tie string at centre of cane

attach canes to cane above, always working from the bottom up

tie on all sorts of objects

pop stars mobile

TWO-WAY PICTURE

1 Choose two coloured magazine pictures. Either make sure they are both exactly the same size, or cut them to the same size.

2 Take a piece of thin card the same height as the magazine cuttings. Fold it into concertina pleats 10 millimetres wide. Cut picture one into 10 millimetre strips.

3 Glue these 10 millimetre strips each in turn onto the left-facing pleats. Cut the second picture into 10 millimetre strips and again glue these in turn onto the right-facing pleats.

If you look at your concertina folder from the left you will see one picture. If you view from the right you will see the other.

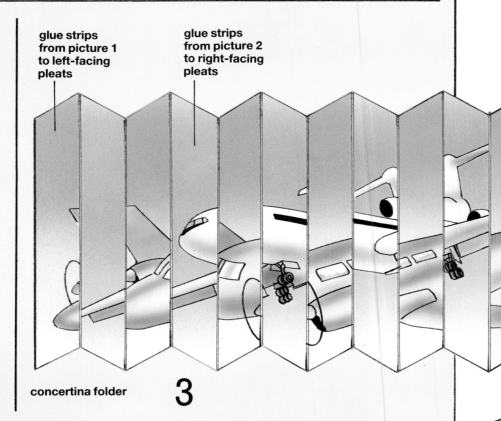

glue strips from picture 1 to left-facing pleats

glue strips from picture 2 to right-facing pleats

concertina folder **3**

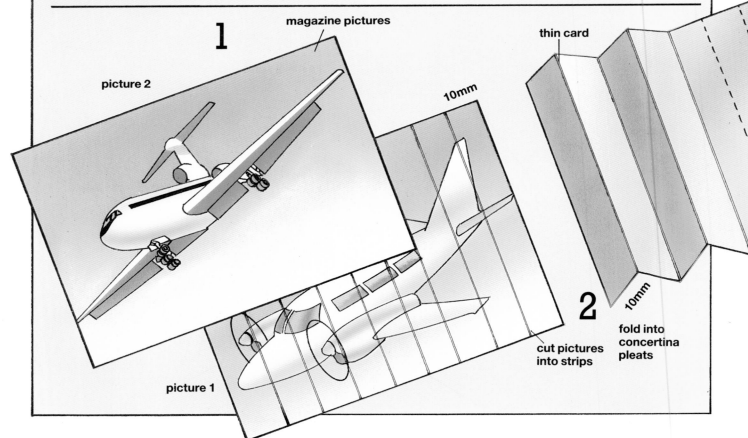

1 magazine pictures

picture 2

10mm

thin card

cut pictures into strips

2 fold into concertina pleats

10mm

picture 1

THREE-WAY PICTURE

1 For this, three magazine pictures are needed. Again they must all be the same size. Number your pictures 1–3.

2 Cut a piece of card to the same height and the total length of the three pictures. Crease the card into 10 millimetre lengths. Number it 1, 2, 3; 1, 2, 3. . . as shown.

3 Bend the card so that it makes the pattern of the folds (X), show.

4 Cut each magazine picture into 10 millimetre strips. Glue strips from your picture 1 to the card wherever the number 1 is shown. You will see that this means gluing the first strip at the edge, missing two strips of card, then gluing the next picture strip in position. Continue gluing one and missing two until you finish picture.

Glue strips from your pictures 2 and 3 in the same way in the positions shown.

5 Fold the concertina so that every third strip remains flat.

View the concertina folder from the left to see one picture, from the front to see another, and from the right to see yet another.

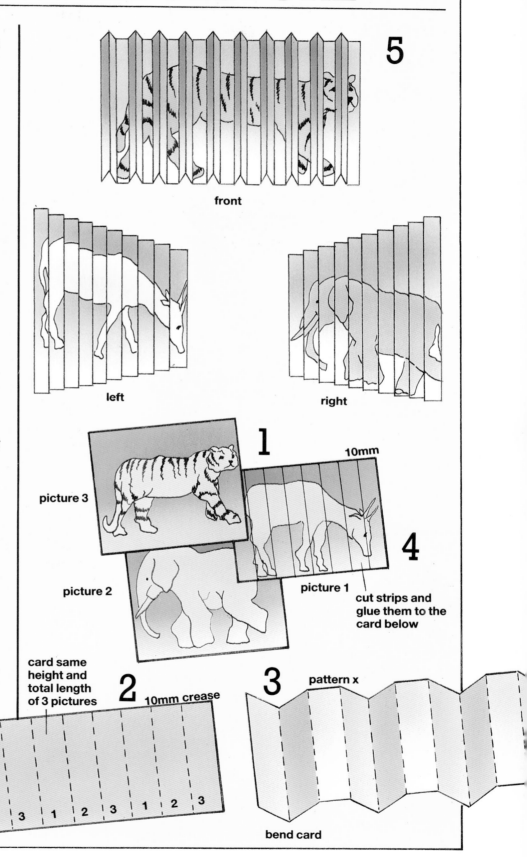

5 front

left

right

1

4

10mm

picture 3

picture 2

picture 1

cut strips and glue them to the card below

card same height and total length of 3 pictures

2 10mm crease

1 2 3 1 2 3 1 2 3 1 2 3

3 pattern x

bend card

POP UP CARDS

Greeting cards that pop up when you open them are very popular.

They are easy to make.

1 Trace the balloon and butterfly onto thin card. Colour them in and cut them out.

2 Trace two copies of the V shape and cut these from card too. Score each V shape along the dotted lines.

3 Take a sheet of thin card and fold it to make your greetings card. Fold and glue your V shape into this folded card as shown.

4 Glue the long 'tail' of the butterfly as illustrated.

5 Attach the balloon by a piece of cotton and glue.

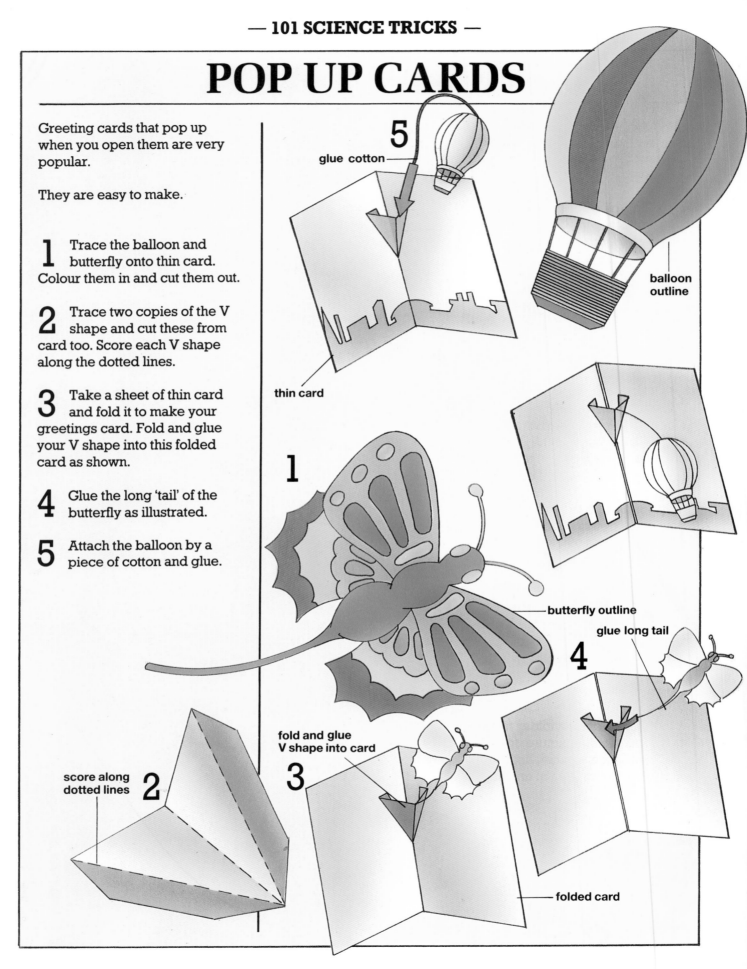

glue cotton

balloon outline

thin card

butterfly outline

glue long tail

score along dotted lines

fold and glue V shape into card

folded card

PICTURE PATTERNS

There was a famous Dutch artist, called M.C. Escher who was fascinated with the way images fitted together. Here are some examples of the sort of pictures he painted. You can see how the images interlink, one with another to cover the whole surface without any overlap or gap. On the next page there are images of birds and ghosts for you to trace and use to make interlinking patterns.

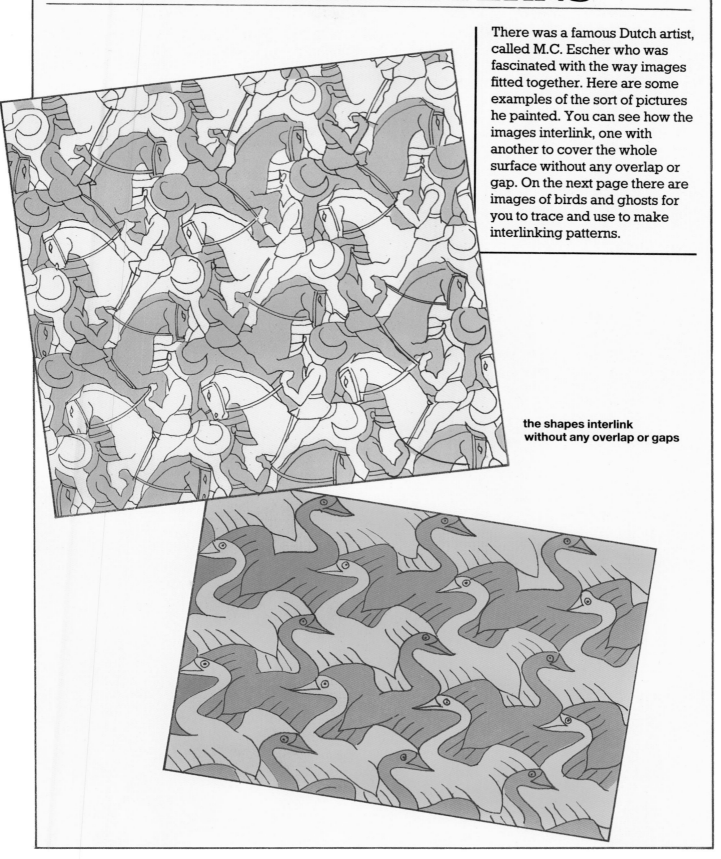

**the shapes interlink
without any overlap or gaps**

BIRDS

1 Trace a number of these birds onto thin card.

2 Colour them in bright colours and cut them out and fit them into an interlinking pattern as M.C. Escher did in his paintings.

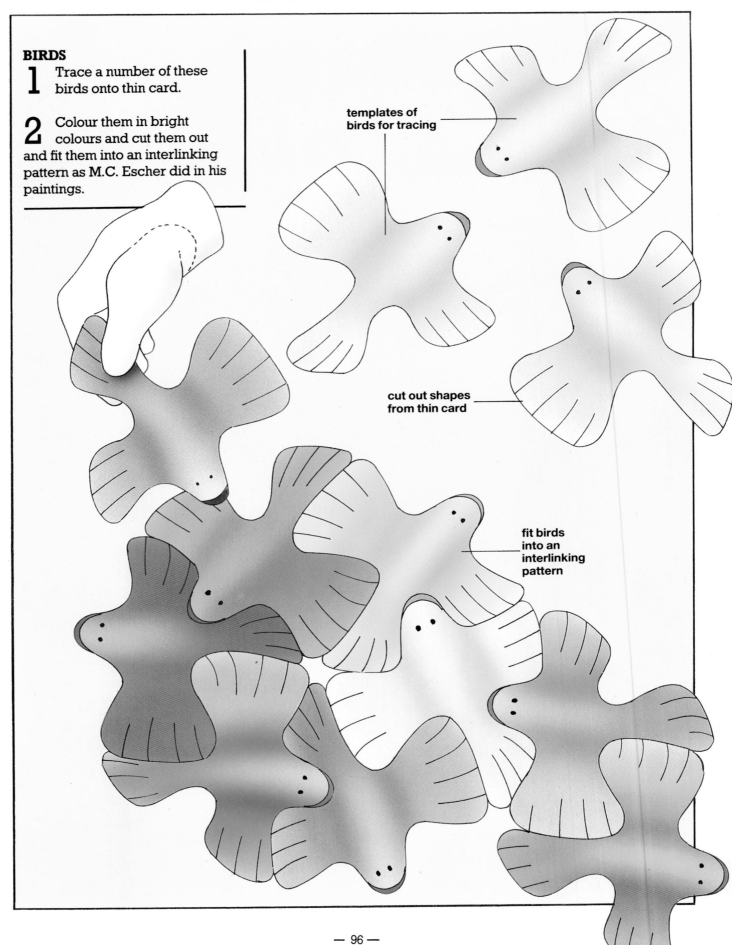

templates of birds for tracing

cut out shapes from thin card

fit birds into an interlinking pattern

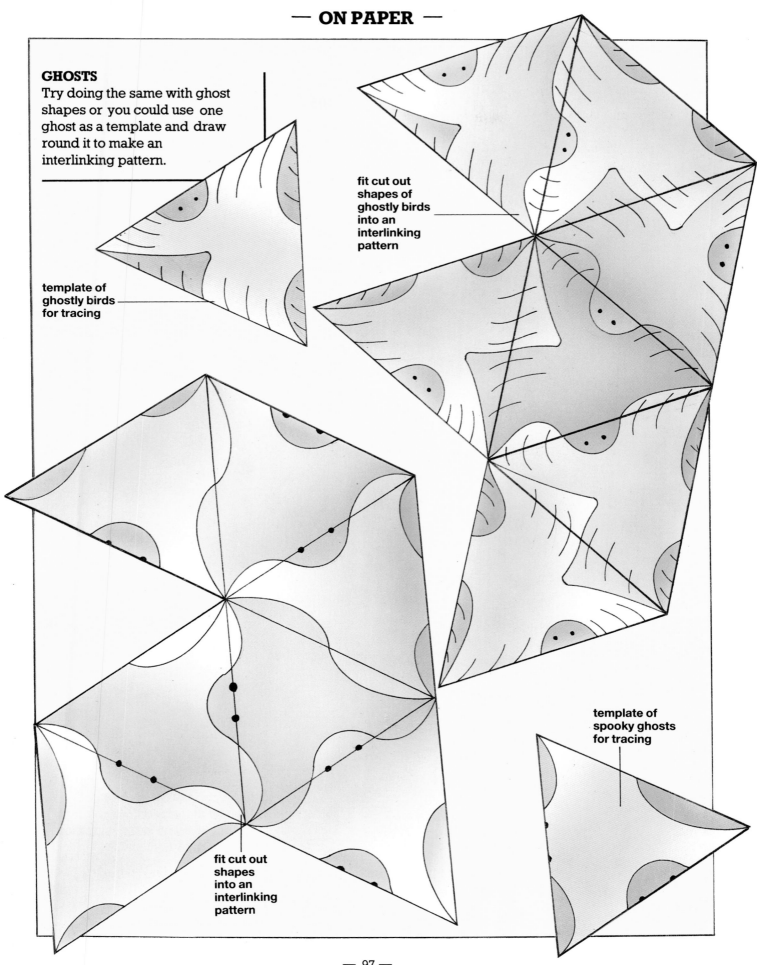

GHOSTS
Try doing the same with ghost shapes or you could use one ghost as a template and draw round it to make an interlinking pattern.

template of ghostly birds for tracing

fit cut out shapes of ghostly birds into an interlinking pattern

template of spooky ghosts for tracing

fit cut out shapes into an interlinking pattern

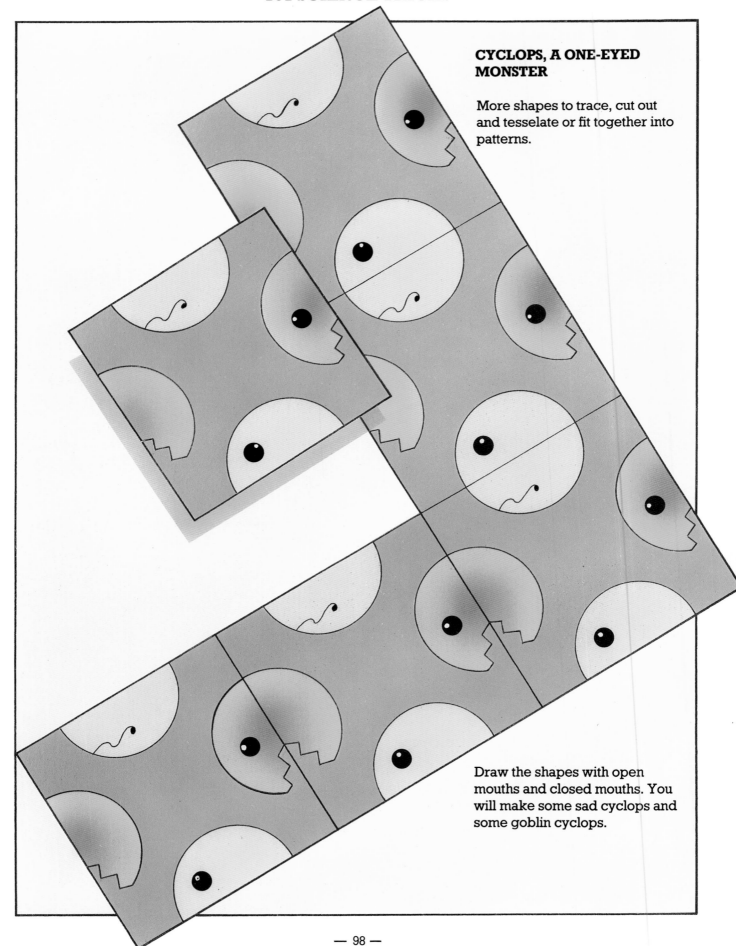

CYCLOPS, A ONE-EYED MONSTER

More shapes to trace, cut out and tesselate or fit together into patterns.

Draw the shapes with open mouths and closed mouths. You will make some sad cyclops and some goblin cyclops.

PLUMBER'S NIGHTMARE

You can make more complex
designs as this pattern shows.

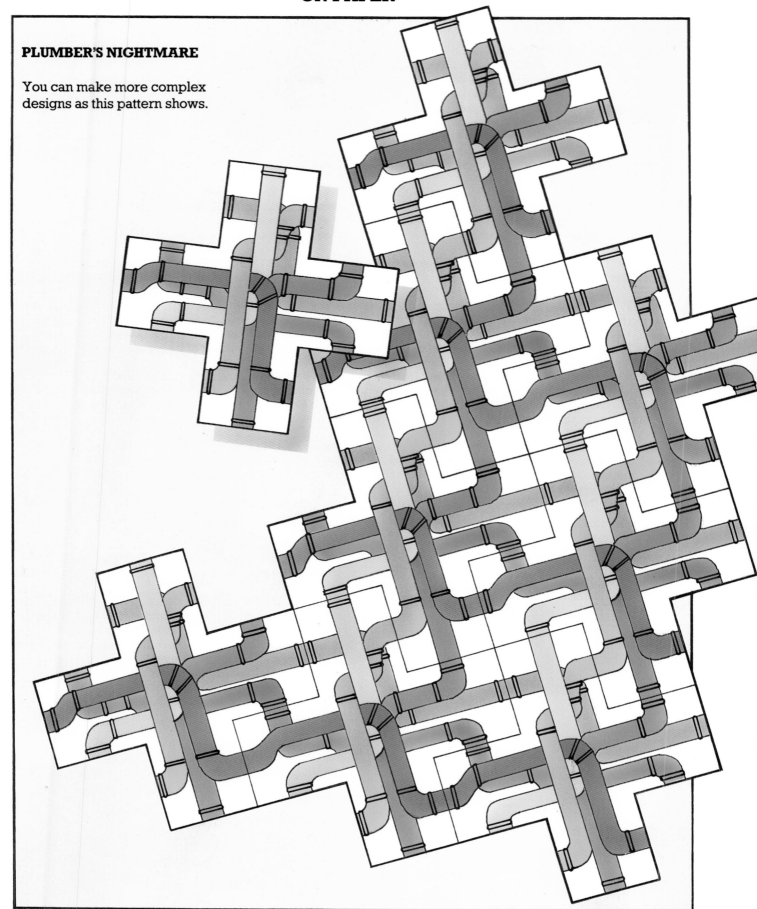

NOTES FOR PARENTS AND TEACHERS

Pages 71 – 75   Things fall because of a force of attraction towards the centre of the earth. We are constantly adjusting our centre of gravity, albeit subconsciously, as we move. However, we originally as very small children had to learn how to do this. These pages are concerned with centre of gravity games and toys, being concerned with how to get a balance about a central point.

Pages 76 – 77   Children are learning that sounds are produced by vibrating objects. You do not get a sound without making something vibrate.

Page 76   The bull roarer vibrates when spun making its peculiar noise.

Page 77   The buzzsaw causes a vibration of the paper making a high pitched sound.

Pages 78 – 79   These pages describe two clocks. In one we tell the time by the sun, in the other by the stars. Children's attention will be drawn to the apparent daily motion of both sun and stars. They will realise that the day length changes throughout the year and be able to measure time using their clocks.

Page 78   The sundial shown is a typical sundial. The raised central portion is called the gnomon. The angle of the gnomon to the horizontal varies with the latitude of where you live. For example in London it is 51.5°, while in New York it is 41°.

The graduations on the sundial are not an equal distance apart.

This table gives their position.

Sundial Time	Angle for London (Latitude 51.5°)
6 am	0
7	19
8	36.5
9	52
10	65.5
11	78
12	90
1 pm	102
2	114.5
3	128
4	143.5
5	161
6	180

You draw the 4 am and 5 am marks diametrically opposite the 4 pm and 5 pm marks; with the 7 pm and 8 pm marks diametrically opposite the 7 am and 8 am ones.

This information is correct for London. In other countries you would need to look up your latitude in an atlas. Make your gnomon to the angle of that latitude. Choose a sunny day! Set up your sundial and plot the angles of the shadows cast on the hour through the day. You could then measure the angles formed and make a table like the one shown above for London.

Page 79   This clock will, of course, rotate anticlockwise since the stars appear to spin in an anti-clockwise manner. In the southern hemisphere you need to choose appropriate constellations.

Pages 80 – 81   Both these models illustrate how warm air rises, that is they work on convection currents.

Pages 82 – 83   Magic squares show how numbers can intrigue and at the same time illustrate how they do not behave in a wayward manner but give pattern. Looking for pattern is at the heart of mathematics.

Pages 84 – 85   Tangrams give children scope for inventing all sorts of patterns and figures, and at the same time help develop the concept of area as amount of surface covered.

Pages 86 – 87   The 3D structures described on these pages are the Platonic solids. They are the only regular solids. They were invented by Plato, and the Greeks used them as symbols: tetrahedron (fire), octahedron (air), cube (earth), icosahedron (water), dodecahedron (universe).

Pages 88 – 91   The cards and the mobiles all use levers as their working principle. That is to say they all use a bar turning about a point.

Pages 92 – 93   Two and three way pictures like these greatly intrigued our Victorian ancestors. Making them draws attention to how our position in relation to objects affects how we see them. Changing our position in relation to the models made on these two pages completely changes the picture we see.

Pages 94   Pop up cards take children into paper engineering.

Pages 95 – 99   Tesselating shapes and picture patterns not only introduce children to the fitting of shapes together but are an early and very important introduction to the concept of area as amount of surface covered.

THINGS NEEDED TO MAKE
THE MODELS

adhesives
card
cardboard
masking tape
paper
pair of compasses
pens, felt tip
protractor
Stanley knife, pocket
ruler
scissors
sticky tape
string, thin, strong

THINGS NEEDED FOR
INDIVIDUAL ACTIVITIES

aeroplane wheels, model
ball, tennis
balloon
balsa wood
balsa glue
bamboo rods
beads
biro, used
bottles, plastic
camphor
candle
canes, garden
clothes peg, clip type
coathanger, wire
coins
compass
corks
cotton
cotton reels
darning needle
drink cans
dowel rods
drinking straws
elastic bands
fan, pocket electric
fishing line, nylon
forks
hacksaw

hammer
hand-drill
hatpin
knitting needles
matchsticks
mirrors, handbag
nails
needles
newspaper
paper, greaseproof tissue
paper-clips
paper fasteners
plaster of Paris
plastic sheeting
plastic container
Plasticine
playing cards
pins, large
popper
propellers
sand
staples
straw, drinking
tray, tin
wire
wool, coloured

INDEX

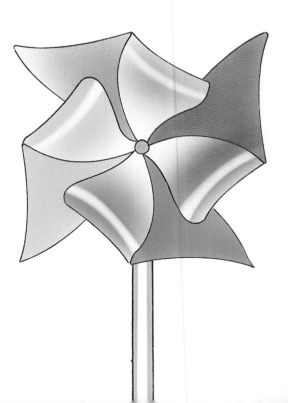